HELPING CHILDREN TO
MANAGE TRANSITIONS

Also part of the Helping Children to Build Wellbeing and Resilience series

Helping Children to Manage Anger
Photocopiable Activity Booklet to Support Wellbeing and Resilience
Deborah M. Plummer
Illustrated by Alice Harper
ISBN 978 1 78775 863 6
eISBN 978 1 78775 864 3

Helping Children to Manage Stress
Photocopiable Activity Booklet to Support Wellbeing and Resilience
Deborah M. Plummer
Illustrated by Alice Harper
ISBN 978 1 78775 865 0
eISBN 978 1 78775 866 7

Using Imagination, Mindful Play and Creative Thinking to Support Wellbeing and Resilience in Children
Deborah M. Plummer
Illustrated by Alice Harper
eISBN 978 1 78775 867 4

Helping Children to Manage Friendships
Photocopiable Activity Booklet to Support Wellbeing and Resilience
Deborah M. Plummer
Illustrated by Alice Harper
ISBN 978 1 78775 868 1
eISBN 978 1 78775 869 8

Helping Children to Build Communication Skills
Photocopiable Activity Booklet to Support Wellbeing and Resilience
Deborah M. Plummer
Illustrated by Alice Harper
ISBN 978 1 78775 870 4
eISBN 978 1 78775 871 1

Helping Children to Build Self-Confidence
Photocopiable Activity Booklet to Support Wellbeing and Resilience
Deborah M. Plummer
Illustrated by Alice Harper
ISBN 978 1 78775 872 8
eISBN 978 1 78775 873 5

Helping Children *to* Manage Transitions

Photocopiable Activity Booklet to Support Wellbeing and Resilience

Deborah M. Plummer

Illustrated by Alice Harper

Jessica Kingsley Publishers
London and Philadelphia

First published in Great Britain in 2022 by Jessica Kingsley Publishers
An imprint of Hodder & Stoughton Ltd
An Hachette Company

Some material was first published in *Using Interactive Imagework with Children* [1998], *Self-Esteem Games for Children* [2006], *Helping Children to Build Self-Esteem* [2007], *Helping Children to Cope with Change, Stress and Anxiety* [2008], *Social Skills Games for Children* [2008], and *Focusing and Calming Games for Children* [2012]. This edition first published in Great Britain in 2022 by Jessica Kingsley Publishers.

1

A CIP catalogue record for this title is available from the British Library and the Library of Congress

ISBN 978 1 78775 861 2
eISBN 978 1 78775 862 9

Printed and bound in Great Britain by Bell & Bain Limited

Jessica Kingsley Publishers' policy is to use papers that are natural, renewable and recyclable products and made from wood grown in sustainable forests. The logging and manufacturing processes are expected to conform to the environmental regulations of the country of origin.

Jessica Kingsley Publishers
Carmelite House
50 Victoria Embankment
London EC4Y 0DZ

www.jkp.com

Contents

Acknowledgements

I have collected or devised the games and activities in this series of books over a 30-year period of working first as a speech and language therapist with children and adults, and then as a lecturer and workshop facilitator. Some were contributed by children during their participation in therapy groups or by teachers and therapists during workshops and discussions. Thank you!

The suggestions for adaptations and the expansion activities have arisen from my experiences of running children's groups. Many of them combine elements of ImageWork (Dr Dina Glouberman), Personal Construct Theory (see, for example, Peggy Dalton and Gavin Dunnett) and Solution-Focused Brief Therapy (Insoo Kim Berg and Steve de Shazer). My thanks therefore go to my teachers and mentors in these fields.

I have also found the following books helpful:

- Arnold, A. (1976) *The World Book of Children's Games*. London: Pan Books Ltd.
- Beswick, C. (2003) *The Little Book of Parachute Play*. London: Featherstone Education Ltd.
- Brandes, D. and Phillips, H. (1979) *Gamesters' Handbook: 140 Games for Teachers and Group Leaders*. London: Hutchinson.
- Dunn, O. (1978) *Let's Play Asian Children's Games*. Macmillan Southeast Asia in association with the Asian Cultural Centre for UNESCO.
- Liebmann, M. (2004) *Art Therapy for Groups: A Handbook of Themes and Exercises* (2nd edition). London and New York: Routledge.
- Masheder, M. (1989) *Let's Play Together*. London: Green Print.
- Neelands, J. (1990) *Structuring Drama Work: A Handbook of Available Forms in Theatre and Drama*. Cambridge: Cambridge University Press.

Note: There are many different non-competitive 'mini' games that can be used for choosing groups, coordinators (leaders) and order of play where appropriate. I have listed several options in the

accompanying eBook Using Imagination, Mindful Play and Creative Thinking to Support Wellbeing and Resilience in Children. *I suggest that the format is varied between sessions so that the children can experiment with different ways of doing this. The choosing then becomes part of the personal learning.*

The following icons are used throughout to indicate the three elements of the IMPACT approach:

Imagination

Mindful Play

Creative Thinking

Introduction

This book is one of a series based on the use of Imagination (I), Mindful Play (MP) and Creative Thinking (CT) to enhance social, psychological and emotional wellbeing and resilience in children. IMPACT activities and strategies encourage children to build life skills through carefully structured and supportive play experiences. Emphasis is given to the important role played by adult facilitators in creating a safe space in which children can share and explore feelings and difficulties and experiment with different ways of thinking and 'being'. This approach is explained in the accompanying eBook *Using Imagination, Mindful Play and Creative Thinking to Support Wellbeing and Resilience in Children*, which also contains many further ideas for games and activities and examples of how the IMPACT approach can enhance daily interactions with children.

Please remember, if you are a parent or carer and you are concerned about ongoing and persistently high levels of anxiety or aggressive behaviour, or persistently low mood in your child, it is always best to seek further support via your child's school or your child's doctor. This book is not intended as a substitute for the professional help that may be needed when children are experiencing clinically recognized difficulties such as chronic school phobia, severe social anxiety or childhood depression. Although all transitions involve some degree of loss, it is also not within the scope of this book to look specifically at change resulting from bereavement.

USING THIS BOOK

The games and activities in this book help children to:

- identify some of their worries and fears about transitions
- build skills and strategies that will help them to cope with times of change
- explore the possible benefits and enjoyment that can sometimes result from change.

The IMPACT approach emphasizes eight *foundation elements* for wellbeing (see the accompanying eBook *Using Imagination, Mindful Play and Creative Thinking to Support Wellbeing and Resilience in Children*). Although all eight of these elements are closely interconnected, the focus for the games and activities in this book centres on two of the elements that are particularly relevant when thinking about transitions: *self-awareness* and *self-confidence*. Here is a reminder of what these two elements encapsulate:

Self-awareness

Self-awareness is the cornerstone of realistic self-evaluation. It involves:

- developing the ability to be focused in the here and now rather than being absorbed in unhelpful thoughts about the past or future; this includes awareness and identification of feelings as they arise
- developing the ability to switch attention appropriately from external events to internal thoughts and feelings and vice versa
- understanding that emotional, mental and physical changes are a natural part of life
- being aware of the normality of a range of feelings and how these link to thoughts and behaviour.

The IMPACT approach offers a forum in which feelings are acknowledged, valued and openly discussed in a non-judgemental way. The games and activities help children to develop the ability to switch attention effectively between internal and external stimuli, cope more effectively with distractions, make informed choices about how and when to focus their attention, monitor their internal 'self-talk' and build effective strategies for self-calming.

Self-confidence

This involves:

- knowing that each person's opinions and thoughts have value, and knowing how to express these appropriately
- feeling strong enough to accept challenges and make personal choices
- developing knowledge and skills in order to be able to experiment with different methods of problem-solving
- being flexible enough to alter coping strategies if needed
- feeling able to cope with the unexpected.

The IMPACT approach offers children the chance to build competence and self-efficacy in a supportive environment. They will be able to experiment with a variety of skills, take on progressively bigger challenges, be creative in constructing and trying out new games, take on different roles within games and cope with unexpected outcomes. Exploring a range of appropriate strategies and becoming familiar with the language of problem-solving is also an important aspect of IMPACT activities.

Facilitator involvement

All the games and activities in this series of books offer opportunities for facilitators to take an active part. Our participation reflects the nature of extended communities and gives us an opportunity to have fun alongside the children. Throughout the games in this book, the term 'game coordinator' therefore refers to either adult or child participants, as appropriate for the level and stage of each group.

Activities

The first section of games and activities, 'IMPACT Essentials for Managing Transitions' (section II), introduces children to the central features of the IMPACT approach – using imagery, being mindful and thinking creatively. There are also activities for group 'gelling' and for exploring relevant concepts such as self-respect and respect for others. Each book in this series has a different set of IMPACT essentials. With a slight change of emphasis, you will therefore be able to use any of these to supplement your sessions if needed.

The remainder of the sections are arranged in accordance with specific aspects of managing transitions: 'Skills and Resources', 'Thinking about Change', 'Making a Change', 'Taking Care of Myself' and 'Reflecting on Change and Setting Goals'. You might also find it useful to add a selection of games and activities from *Helping Children to Manage Stress*, which is available in this series.

The creative potential for supporting skill development is one of the wonderful features of childhood games. I have given several suggestions for specific skills that might be learned or further developed during each game and its associated activities, but these are not exhaustive. You may want to add more to suit your own focus of work.

Ideas are also suggested for adaptations. These illustrate some of the many ways in which a basic game or activity can be simplified or made more complex to suit diverse developmental levels, strengths and learning differences.

Reflection and discussion

Another important aspect of all the games and activities is the opportunity they provide for children to expand their thinking skills. To aid this process, I have included suggestions for further reflection and discussion ('Talk about'). These include a mixture of possible prompt questions and suggestions for comments or explanations that can be useful when introducing or elaborating some of the ideas. (See Chapter 11, 'Mindful Communication', and Chapter 13, 'Mindful Praise and Appreciation', in *Using Imagination, Mindful Play and Creative Thinking to Support Wellbeing and Resilience in Children* for more ideas about facilitating discussions with children.) You may want to select just a couple of these or spread the discussion over several sessions.

These discussion topics also provide an opportunity for drawing links between different themes at later times. You could remind children of particular games or activities when this is relevant: 'Do you remember when we played that game of... What did you find out about listening...?' or 'How might the resilience tree be useful to us in this situation?'

Expansion activities

Most of the main games and activities are followed by one or more expansion activities. These are an important part of the process too. They encourage children to recognize the benefits of a stepped approach to learning and to the process of change, understand how new skills can build on previous experiences, and understand how current skills can be strengthened.

Activity sheets

Some of the expansion activities have accompanying activity sheets that can also be adapted for discussion, these can be found in section VIII. I have found that children particularly like to draw or write about their imaginary world. Their drawings and jottings might then be the starting point for wellbeing stories (see *Using Imagination, Mindful Play and Creative Thinking to Support Wellbeing and Resilience in Children* for ideas about how to create these stories). They can also be made into a personal 'Book of Wisdom' and perhaps act as reminders of some of the strategies that children might want to use again in the future.

Note: Please keep in mind that IMPACT activity sheets are offered as supplementary material to expand and reinforce each child's learning experiences. They are not intended as stand-alone alternatives to the mindful play and supportive discussions that are central to the IMPACT approach.

Exploring Transitions

You will perhaps be familiar with all or some of the following parental concerns:

> Kaushika is crying every night and saying that she doesn't want to go to school, but I know that the teachers are really nice, and she's got some good friends. I can't understand what's wrong.

> Terri worries about just about everything! Even the smallest change in her routine upsets her. She makes herself physically sick sometimes with her worrying.

> We've been posted to another new place. The children have only just got settled in at school and I'm concerned that another move is going to be really difficult for them.

> When his best friend moved away he seemed to go inside himself for months. Now he's mixing with a group of kids who are real trouble-makers. I can't get him to see that they're not good friends to have.

In the context of this book, *transition* is seen as the period of time when a child is facing an important change, or has already started to experience a change, but is not yet fully established in the new 'territory'. This might be a conscious, self-initiated change or change brought about by circumstances or by natural growth and development. Common examples of transitions for children are starting school, moving from infant to junior education, moving from late childhood to adolescence, moving from one class to another, moving home, changing friendship groups, changing family structures (for example, when parents separate or two families join together, or a new sibling arrives), perhaps even changing roles within the family, such as taking on part of the responsibilities for looking after a younger sibling or becoming a carer for a parent.

A MINDFUL PLAY PERSPECTIVE

The IMPACT approach to helping children manage transitions is based on child-centred, mindful play interactions. It reflects the view that children benefit from being involved in the process of change without being given overwhelming responsibility for decisions. In other words, they take an active part. They make their own contributions while at the same time benefiting from the mindful care of adults who will support them before, during and after a change, and who will help them to build resilience for future challenges.

In order to get a feel for some of the games and activities in this book and how these relate to a child's experience of transitions, I believe that it is helpful to start from our own perspectives. How do we, as adults, deal with transitions in our own lives? How do we already support the children in our care as they negotiate these tricky times? How can we maximize this support? Experiencing the following activities from an adult perspective will also undoubtedly trigger some thoughts about how you can adapt these and other activities in this book. There are no right or wrong answers; they are simply ways of exploring the topic.

Begin by setting aside a short period of uninterrupted time when you will have the opportunity to carry out and to reflect on a single activity – 10–15 minutes is probably ample. I suggest that you only do one activity and then go back to doing other things. Please don't be tempted to do all the activities one after the other in a single sitting, even if you have the time. A period of reflection is always useful after an exploratory activity.

Exploratory activity 1.1. The experience of change

Think of a time of transition in your life when you have made a small or moderately manageable change. This may have been through your own choice or through circumstances that were not in your control. Do you remember how you felt about this change at the time? Were there any surprises? Were there any frustrations? Did this change lead to any other changes? Did anything stay the same? What is the strongest feeling that you have in relation to this change now? Has the way in which you manage transitions altered over time? On a scale of 1–5, where 1 is 'I'm starting to build my skills' and 5 is 'I'm very confident', how confident do you feel about managing any future transitions?

We know that the ways in which children cope with transitions will differ according to both external circumstances, such as support from others, and personal resources, such as healthy self-esteem and effective stress management strategies. Of course, the younger the child, the fewer personal resources they are likely to have.

Experiencing many small changes can often help children to build these skills and resources and to manage a large change successfully, particularly if they are also well supported by key adults. Such experiences will usually result in increased confidence and resilience. Nevertheless, transitions at any age (particularly major transitions) can affect us at a much deeper level than outward circumstances alone might sometimes suggest. This is because transitions often also involve adjustments in self-concept, perceptions of control in one's life and feelings of self-efficacy. For children, who are still in the process of 'inventing' themselves and finding their way in the world, this can be especially unsettling. Our own non-judgemental acknowledgement of the range of possible emotions engendered by transition periods can be of significant help in deciding how and where to focus our support.

Two of the most notable ways in which children might experience transitions are as a significant loss or as an imminent threat.

Any change in circumstances, personal development or beliefs, thoughts or behaviours automatically entails an element of loss. This loss of the familiar means that children may no longer be able to predict what will happen with the same degree of confidence. This, in turn, may lead to the escalation of worries including those that might normally be dealt with quite quickly. For example, a child moves to a different area and a larger school. What will happen if they ask for help in finding their way around? Will they feel foolish? For an already anxious child this could become a major anticipated source of anxiety and lead to further stress. It may also result in sadness related to the loss of 'the way things were'. Such feelings may persist until the new situation becomes the familiar.

Transitions can sometimes lead to children feeling under pressure to change themselves in some way (become more responsible, more brave, less talkative), or to see themselves or the world as suddenly and unexpectedly different ('I've always thought of myself as brave, but suddenly everything feels scary'). This may result in a child experiencing feelings that are more commonly associated with actual or anticipated physical threat. A threat to their self-concept or concept of the world can be extremely uncomfortable for some children and may manifest as fear, panic or anger. There may also be feelings of guilt.

Feelings of guilt may be evident if a child feels that they are about to step outside, or have already stepped outside, their 'picture' of themselves. As an example, a child who sees themselves as quiet and hard-working might find themselves in a situation where this concept is challenged. Let's say they are drawn into a more boisterous group in order to fit in with the children in their new neighbourhood. Perhaps this results in 'being in trouble'. The underlying feeling of guilt in this situation might be totally disproportionate to the actual circumstances. The child's experience of this particular transition to a new home is then overlaid with more complex feelings that could, in turn, lead to further anxiety.

Once again, the intensity of feeling will naturally be influenced by the developmental stage of a child and their available internal and external resources, but certainly for some children, frequent changes can lead to feelings associated with loss and threat much more easily than for others. Added to this, the uncertainties that exist in a child's world may have already been amplified by events such as the pandemic of 2020/21 (the world is friendly/not friendly, meeting new people is okay/not okay).

The next activity is derived from Personal Construct Theory.[1] It is useful for looking at personal change and for examining difficulties in making a decision between two alternatives. As you will see, the principles behind this are also relevant to transitions during childhood.

Exploratory activity 1.2. The ABC of change

First identify a change or potential change that is causing you a dilemma of some sort. Once again, please choose something minor!

Let's say you are thinking about changing your internet provider or changing the furniture in your living room or increasing the amount of exercise that you do.

Divide a piece of paper into four sections and label each section as below. Leave room at the top to write the dilemma that you are exploring. Write this down under the heading A1.

A1	A2
B1 Disadvantages	B2 Advantages
C1 Advantages	C2 Disadvantages

---

1   See, for example, Dalton, P. and Dunnett, G. (2005) *A Psychology for Living: Personal Construct Theory for Professionals and Clients* (2nd edition). Chichester: John Wiley & Sons Ltd.

Find the opposite of this and write it down under A2. So, for example, you might write 'Continue to do my current level of exercise' under A1 and 'Join a gym' under A2.

Write down the *disadvantages* of A1. Think of as many as possible.

Now list the *advantages* of A2.

Your lists will probably seem fairly obvious to you – writing lists of pros and cons is a common way of approaching decisions about personal change.

Now think about the *advantages* of A1 (your present situation). This highlights the 'payoffs' of staying as you are.

Under A2 write down the *disadvantages* of changing.

Now look at the whole table and ask yourself:

- Do I still want to make the change?
- If I still want to make this change, is there any way of achieving it without losing some of the advantages I am experiencing at the moment?
- Is there a way in which I can reach a compromise?
- How can I resolve any dilemmas that this has shown up?

When you have completed this, you may have a better indication of why it is difficult to make certain changes. Are there any insights gained from this activity that you feel could be useful when supporting children through times of transition?

IMPACT adaptation for children

Invite the children to draw a picture of themselves in the current situation, before a planned change (or in their previous situation, before a recent change happened). Gently encourage as much detail as possible, including people, objects, feelings and so on. Try to keep your input to a minimum while they are drawing. You might make observational comments when they have finished, such as 'I can see you have drawn a smiley "you" in the playground with your friend'.

Ask the child: 'If this picture had a title, what would it be?'

Invite a second picture that shows the anticipated or recent change (new school, new house, new sibling, etc.). Ask the child: 'What would be the title for this picture?'

Look at both pictures side by side. Is there a person, object or representation of a feeling that can be taken from the first picture that would help the child to feel different in the second situation? Ask them to draw this into the second picture.

Talk about how this might translate into the actual situation. Once again, it is helpful to keep your questions to a minimum, to phrase them in the positive and to reflect back the child's own words. For example, if a child is feeling sad, you might ask them: 'When you are no longer feeling sad all the time, what feeling will you have instead?' If the child says 'bouncy' then you could explore this further: 'What could you take with you from the first picture that would help you to feel bouncy in this new picture/situation?'

Occasionally, you might find that something *unhelpful* from the first picture is already absent from the second one, and this can also offer important insights.

Exploratory activity 1.3. Motivation for change

Knowing what motivates us to engage with change helps us to make more conscious choices and helps in the long-term management of transitions. Each of us will be motivated in different ways, so personal relevance is a key factor.

Think of five or six motivators that might lead you to make changes in your life (such as having fun, relationships with others or personal success). Can you think of a similar number of motivators that would be relevant for a particular child or group of children? Note any obvious differences and similarities in your lists.

Because children face many changes that are not self-initiated, even a small element of perceived gain can help them to engage. I am not advocating bribery here ('If you do this, I will buy you a new bike!'), but there may well be an element of gain inherent in the change itself – for example, if a child is motivated by having more time to be with family or friends, perhaps a house move will offer them that opportunity because they will be closer to school, or because parents will not have to commute so far to work.

Our own reassurances will, of course, help children to negotiate changes, and it is worth thinking about how you might offer such reassurance before, during and after particular events. I suggest this because I know that we might very easily try to reassure children with quite vague thoughts such as 'You'll be fine', 'Don't worry' or 'It will only feel strange on the first day'. Most children will need something more concrete than this to allay any fears they might have, and this may need some preparation on our part. For example, you might start by acknowledging their fears and worries and assuring them that these are normal. You could talk about some of the most important things that children will need to know about a particular change, and reassure them about those aspects that will stay the same or that will only change very gradually.

You may also want to set aside a regular time when children can ask questions about an upcoming change or about a new situation that has already occurred. Or you might want to keep reassuring them that they will be able to ask questions at *any* time if they are unsure about anything ('8. The worry box' could be used or adapted for this). Which would work best for you and for the children? Perhaps they need to have both options.

By taking time to think about transitions in this way you will have 'nudged' a few memories and thoughts to the surface of your awareness.

The next activity takes this one step further and shows how imagination can play an important role in how we feel and what we do in relation to change.[2]

Exploratory activity 1.4. Imagining a change

In order to avoid distractions, this activity will be maximally effective if you read through the guidance a couple of times and then carry out the activity with your eyes closed. I suggest that you also have some paper and pencils close to hand.

> Think of one small thing that you would like to change or that is about to change. For example, you are going to join a new art class, or you are considering starting a meditation group. Settle yourself in a comfortable position... Allow your eyes to close gently. Follow the normal pattern of your breathing for a moment... Notice the flow of air in and out of your body... Now let that focus fade...
>
> Imagine that it is a specified time in the future and your intended change has already taken place. Everything has gone well. You are pleased with the outcome. In your imagination, notice where you are and what you are doing. Take time to feel what this is like. Engage all your senses.
>
> Remember in all this to use your 'memory' from the future, *as if it has already happened*, not your 'thoughts' about what it might be like.

When you are ready, ask yourself the following questions, giving yourself plenty of time to explore each one:

- What exactly is the good feeling that I have?

---

2   See, for example, www.dinaglouberman.com

- How does my body feel?
- How do I feel mentally now that this change has happened?
- How do I feel emotionally?
- Looking back, what was the attitude that got me here?
- What did I do that meant that this worked well? What do I remember doing before and during the situation that led to such a positive outcome?
- What was I thinking before and during the situation?
- What is the best thing that has happened?
- What has most surprised me now that I have made this change?
- What will happen next?

Spend a few moments enjoying the physical, emotional and mental feelings of having achieved your desired results. When you are ready, open your eyes gently and look at something in your immediate environment. Look at this for a moment as if you have never seen it before. Now move your attention to something else in your environment – a sound or an object. When you feel fully back in your current environment, take time to make a note of your experience (or sketch something that captures the essence of your experience). Do you have any advice for yourself?

In this activity you explored positive feelings and images associated with change. How often might we only look at the worst-case scenarios and imagine ourselves failing or unhappy in our new situation? How much more often might anxious children do this? And to what extent might these negative forward projections culminate in actual discomfort or unhappiness and lead to resistance to change? Experimenting with different (realistic) future possibilities will help children to break patterns of thinking and behaviour that are unhelpful to their wellbeing and will open the opportunity for more creativity in how they cope with future challenges. Through imagery children can face some of their fears and put them more into perspective. In order to overcome unwanted feelings of anxiety they can be helped to 'reframe' an impending change ('What if you had already done this? See yourself making the change. What is happening?'). They can be encouraged to look at their dilemmas from different perspectives, explore what it would be like to act in a different way, or reach a compromise in order to make the change more manageable for themselves.

RELEVANCE FOR IMPACT GAMES AND ACTIVITIES

In summary, IMPACT activities facilitate the learning and consolidation of specific skills that will help children to build resilience and enhance their experiences of wellbeing. Engagement with the activities can be seen as 'experiments' in changing thoughts and behaviour. They ease the process of conscious choice and open up possibilities for children to alter their perceptions of themselves without triggering extremes of uncomfortable feelings. Learning takes place within the safety of a well-structured group or individual support session before children try out new skills and strategies in everyday life. This will help them to assimilate changes more comfortably and to build further skills for the future.

IMPACT Essentials for Managing Transitions

By doing the activities in this section you will be helping children to:

- think about different aspects of themselves, not just how they are dealing with any current difficulties
- put specific changes into a broader context
- see themselves as active participants in change
- begin to explore how the ability to imagine can be a helpful resource
- explore the idea that feelings can change and that we can have some control over them
- continue to develop or consolidate their skills in focusing and attending.

1. The rule of the realm

Wellbeing focus:

☑ Self-confidence   ☑ Self-awareness

Examples of personal skills learned or consolidated:

☑ Listening   ☑ Problem-solving
☑ Cooperation   ☑ Observation
☑ Memory strategies

Examples of general/social learning:

☑ Understanding how rules are made   ☑ Understanding specific rules about the structure and content of games
☑ Understanding rules made by other people

This game encourages players to work together in order to solve a puzzle about group rules. It is a good warm-up or group 'gelling' game, and can also lead into discussions about change, such as changing schools or changing friendship or family groups where 'rules' might be the same or some rules might be different.

How to play
Divide the group into two. Group A leaves the room. Group B makes up a 'talking rule' such as 'Every time you speak you must cross your arms' or 'Every time you finish speaking you must scratch your head'. The game coordinator checks that everyone in Group B remembers to do this by asking each one a simple question such as 'Do you like chocolate?' or 'How old are you?' Group A returns to the room and the coordinator repeats the previous questions or asks similar ones while Group A observes. The aim is for Group A to guess the rule. The emphasis is on group problem-solving – if one person in Group A guesses the correct rule, this means that the whole group has achieved. The children can therefore be encouraged to confer before they guess the rule.

Adaptations

- Allow a maximum of five guesses.
- Rules for older and very able children can be quite complex, such as 'When the coordinator asks you a question it is the person on your left who answers' or 'You have to use the last word from the question to start your answer'.
- All the children stay in the room and the coordinator chooses a place to set up their kingdom, for example 'the moon', 'the playground'. Each person says what they will bring if they are chosen to be part of the new kingdom. The rule that they have to discover either relates to the first letter of their own name or to the first letter of the place where the kingdom will be. The coordinator starts by giving a few examples such as '**S**andip would be welcome in the new kingdom if he brought **s**nakes with him but not if he brought **m**oney. **M**iriam would be welcome if she brought **m**oney, but definitely not if she brought jewels'. The coordinator tells the children if they can join the kingdom or not according to what they offer to bring with them. This needs a strict time limit, and therefore clues may need to be made more and more obvious to give everyone the chance to guess the 'rule' and join the kingdom! The children can be encouraged to help each other out towards the end of the game in order to ensure that no one is left out.

Talk about

Why do games have rules? Do all groups need rules? Why/why not? Are some rules more useful than others? Can you think of a time or a situation when a rule might change? If you could change one rule in your favourite game, what would it be? Why? What are the most important things to think about when we want to change the rules of a game?

When might a new rule be needed in a group? Think of all the groups that you take part in (for example, family, sports, friends, class). Do the different groups have different rules? Why is that? What rules shall we have for this group?

What is the difference between a suggestion, a rule and a law? What does it feel like to not know a group rule when it seems like everyone else knows it? What could groups do about that? What could you do in that situation?

Thinking about the change(s) you are making, are there any new suggestions or rules that have changed? If so, have they changed a little bit or a lot?

What do you think about having rules for listening or rules for sitting still? When might such rules be useful? When might they not be useful?

EXPANSION ACTIVITY 1.1. CHANGE RULES!

Make up a short story or a poem about a town or a kingdom where there is a rule about change, such as 'Every month all families must move into another house on the same street' or 'No one is ever allowed to change schools'. What happens? The funnier the outcome, the better! Try doing this by taking turns to say one sentence at a time (or even one word at a time). The game coordinator can take responsibility for starting and completing the story or poem. (See *Using Imagination, Mindful Play and Creative Thinking to Support Wellbeing and Resilience in Children* for ideas about constructing wellbeing stories.)

2. Figure me out!

Wellbeing focus:

☑ Self-confidence   ☑ Self-awareness

Examples of personal skills learned or consolidated:

☑ Understanding metaphors   ☑ Observation
☑ Concentration

Examples of general/social learning:

☑ Building self-respect and respect   ☑ Exploring self-concept and
   for others   self-efficacy
☑ Understanding diversity   ☑ Development of body awareness
☑ Developing sensitivity to   and positive body image
   other people's strengths and
   differences

This requires some preparation by the game coordinator beforehand.

How to play

Divide the group into two. Groups A and B then work in different rooms or in different parts of the same room but must not look at what the other group is doing. Within each group the children work in pairs or threes to draw round each other's body outline on large pieces of paper. Each child uses pictures from comics, catalogues, magazines, etc. to 'clothe' their body outline with things that represent something about who they are and what they like to do.

Group A tries to guess who each of the pictures belongs to in Group B and vice versa.

Adaptations

- Once the clothes have been stuck on, add words, headlines and catch-phrases to represent personality strengths.
- Younger children can draw themselves engaged in a favourite activity or

draw around each other's body shapes, or this can be done by a helper. They then add a face, colour in the clothes and add one 'favourite' item such as a football or favourite toy.

Talk about

How did you work out which figure represented which person? Did you discover anything about another person that you hadn't known before? When you look at all the figures, can you see anything that any of them have in common? What are the main differences? Which aspect(s) of your own picture would you most like other people to remember?

EXPANSION ACTIVITY 2.1. I AM ME

Invite the children to draw pictures or write about themselves (see activity sheet 2.1). You might also want to use the magic mirror or portrait frame in Appendix C in the accompanying eBook *Using Imagination, Mindful Play and Creative Thinking to Support Wellbeing and Resilience in Children*.

This self-characterization exercise is based on an idea developed by Personal Construct therapists and psychologists.[1] Writing or drawing a self-characterization can reveal important themes about how children see themselves, what worries them, what they enjoy doing and so on. Some children may find this exercise quite difficult, having little idea of how others might see them. They may need prompts such as: 'What would your best friend say about the way that you…?', 'What helps you to feel happy?' There is no need to filter ideas at this stage. Accept whatever children tell you, even if you disagree with their perceptions.

This activity can be repeated later on, when you feel that the children are beginning to make some noticeable changes in the way that they think and act in difficult situations. Portraits can be drawn at different stages. For example, when a child has successfully coped with an important change, they might draw themselves with a different expression, wearing different clothes or perhaps holding something or doing something that shows what they have achieved.

---

1   See, for example, Fransella, F. and Dalton, P. (2000) *Personal Construct Counselling in Action* (2nd edition). London, Thousand Oaks, CA, and New Delhi: SAGE Publications.

Display the portraits on a wall or keep them in a journal or a special folder that can be used for all the activity sheets and drawings that you do together.

Talk about

What do you most like about being you? What do you love to do? What skills do you have that help you to love doing this? Can any of these skills help you to manage big changes (for example, problem-solving, observation skills, stamina, memory)? How are you different to a year ago? What has changed the most?

Note: Building on a child's current strengths and skills is an important aspect of the IMPACT approach and features in other games throughout this book. See also Using Imagination, Mindful Play and Creative Thinking to Support Wellbeing and Resilience in Children *for further ideas and activities related to this theme.*

EXPANSION ACTIVITY 2.2. IS THIS HOW YOU SEE ME?

Ask the children to collect six descriptions of themselves that they like (words or phrases used by other people to describe them). Encourage a selection of physical descriptions (blue eyes, curly hair, etc.) and descriptions of personality/temperament (happy, bouncy, mischievous, etc.).

Talk about

How accurate do you think these perceptions are? If your grandmother/teacher/uncle says you are artistic or confident, how much would you agree with this?

Sometimes we think that someone feels a certain way, but this may not be how they actually see themselves. For example, a child might appear to others to be very clever, but might think that they are not clever compared to an older brother or sister. Is one observation 'more right' than another, or just a different way of looking at things?

3. Feeling good about being me

Wellbeing focus:

☑ Self-confidence　　　　　　　☑ Self-awareness

Examples of personal skills learnt or consolidated:

☑ Listening　　　　　　　　　☑ Physical coordination
☑ Focusing attention

Examples of general/social learning:

☑ Development of body awareness　☑ Exploring self-concept and
　 and positive body image　　　　 self-efficacy

I suggest that you try this activity for yourself before using it with the children. See if you can all use your imagination to help you to stretch further than you thought you could. The children start by sitting in a comfortable position on the floor or on top of a parachute.

(Please remember, as with all games involving the use of equipment, parachute games should be supervised by an adult at all times. See the notes on equipment in the accompanying eBook *Using Imagination, Mindful Play and Creative Thinking to Support Wellbeing and Resilience in Children*.)

Let's imagine!

Slowly take three full breaths – in through your nose and out through your mouth... Imagine that you are a cat. When cats have been sitting still for a while, or when they have been asleep, they like to stretch out from their noses to their tails... See if you can stretch like a cat. Kneel down with your hands on the floor in front of you... Gradually begin to stretch your arms forward, walking your hands along the floor...feel your body getting longer and longer...

　　Now bring your hands back to just in front of you and start to stretch out your legs behind you instead. First one and then the other... Now lie on your back on the floor and stretch out your arms, spread your fingers as wide as they'll go...

Stretch out your legs and point your toes toward the other side of the room... Now let everything relax again... Gently roll over onto your side and then very slowly sit up.

Now curl yourself up into a ball, and when I say 'go', uncurl and stand up, reach up towards the ceiling as high as you can, really stretching your fingers upwards and standing on tiptoes. 'Go.' Well done! Now relax again and slowly curl up into a ball.

I am going to show you how clever your mind is. Instead of really stretching this time, *imagine* that you are uncurling and reaching for the ceiling. You can reach right up way above your head. You can touch the ceiling. You're so good at stretching you can go much further than you thought was possible. In your imagination feel what it's like to stretch that far... See yourself doing it...

Now...are you ready? *Really* uncurl and stretch up and see how far you go... Stretch...stretch... When you imagined doing this you told your body that it could stretch much further than the first time you did it...and it's working!

Now relax and then give yourself a little shake all over. Shake your arms and your hands. Shake your legs and your feet, shake your shoulders, shake your body...and...sit down.

Talk about

Feeling good about who you are is really important. There are lots of things that happen to us and around us that help us to feel okay about ourselves, but sometimes things happen that are not so nice, and then we might start to think 'I can't do this' or 'I'm no good at this' or 'Everyone has more friends than me'. If this happens, then your imagination can help you to feel better about yourself again *and* it can help you to actually get better at doing some of the hard things.

EXPANSION ACTIVITY 3.1. THINGS I WOULD LIKE TO ACHIEVE

Each child makes a list or draws three things that they would like to achieve (see activity sheet 3.1). These might be achievements related to change and/or general achievements. Sometimes children end up with a mixture of realistic aims and some that are not achievable within the time that you spend together. This can be discussed so that they can choose which aims to focus on. Try to avoid being overly realistic at this point – even amazing dreams for the future can be acknowledged as an exciting thought!

Make brightly coloured stars, flags or badges to help young children to recognize and celebrate their achievements. These can be more motivating than stickers because they can be uniquely personalized. Older children might prefer simple verbal praise. It is always worthwhile experimenting with different reward and praise strategies so that children find it truly motivating to be praised. Praise for strategies well remembered. Acknowledge times of making a 'wise choice' and times of solving a problem. (See further notes on praise in *Using Imagination, Mindful Play and Creative Thinking to Support Wellbeing and Resilience in Children*.)

Talk about
Sometimes other people don't notice or don't know how we feel or what we've achieved. Just because they don't praise us doesn't mean that we didn't do well. Can you think of a time when you have felt good about something even though no one else knew about it? Think of some ways that we might reward or praise ourselves.

4. Sound tracking

Wellbeing focus:

☑ Self-confidence   ☑ Self-awareness

Examples of personal skills learned or consolidated:

☑ Listening   ☑ Describing location
☑ Controlling focus of attention

Examples of general/social learning:

☑ Reducing impulsivity and   ☑ Extending awareness
   building persistence

How to play

Players sit silently in the centre of a darkened room with their eyes closed. The game coordinator hides a clock in the room. Each player tries to locate the clock through listening only. The player who is the most accurate in their description of where the clock is ('Next to the door, on top of the bookcase') takes the next turn to hide the clock. In a small group everyone can be given the opportunity to do this.

Adaptations

- The clock is hidden before the players enter the room.
- Blindfolded players all point in the direction of the clock at the same time. The game coordinator decides who is the most accurate.
- Two clocks are placed in different locations and the players have to find both of them.
- Players take turns to work in pairs to find the clock.
- Instead of a clock, use a hidden recording to play music very quietly.
- Players sit with their eyes closed and try to identify as many different sounds as possible, such as a ticking clock, the sound of breathing, traffic noises outside, rain on the window.
- To make this a visual game, use two identical objects. Show the players one

of these and tell them that the other has been placed in view in the room somewhere. Players all stand or sit on one side of the room and see if they can spot the identical object without moving.

Talk about

How easy or difficult is it to sit very still and listen? What makes it easier? What makes it harder?

Did you hear noises that you hadn't noticed before? When is it useful to be able to choose what we listen to and ignore other sounds around us? What might make this difficult?

What sounds do you like to listen to? What sounds in the environment don't you like?

Put your hands over your ears. What can you hear? Cup your hands over your ears so that you can hear sounds behind you. Now try cupping your hands over your ears so that you can hear sounds in front of you. What do you notice?

EXPANSION ACTIVITY 4.1. MIRRORS

The children sit opposite each other in pairs and take turns to mirror each other's hand movements.

Note: Playing both '4. Sound tracking' and 'Expansion activity 4.1. Mirrors' offers an opportunity to talk with the children about the different types of focusing needed for listening and for observing and also for activities that involve joint attention (see Chapter 7, 'Helping Children to Be Mindful', in Using Imagination, Mindful Play and Creative Thinking to Support Wellbeing and Resilience in Children).

You might also want to use the 'Mindful breathing' activity and/or the 'Mindful musical chairs' game at this point. Both of these activities can be found in *Using Imagination, Mindful Play and Creative Thinking to Support Wellbeing and Resilience in Children* ('Mindful breathing' is in Appendix A; see also Jo and Sarah's reflection on the group games in Chapter 16). These activities also feature in *Helping Children to Manage Stress* (activities 13 and 15).

5. Who walked past?

This is based on a game from Singapore.[2]

Wellbeing focus:

☑ Self-confidence   ☑ Self-awareness

Examples of personal skills learned or consolidated:

☑ Listening   ☑ Focusing attention
☑ Deduction

Examples of general/social learning:

☑ Understanding empathy   ☑ Adaptability
☑ Exploring links between   ☑ Dramatic awareness
  thoughts, feelings and actions

How to play

Player A is the catcher. Player B is the caller. All other players stand to one side of Player B. The catcher wears a blindfold and sits on the floor with the caller standing behind them. The caller calls out a character or animal, for example 'An old man walking with a stick' or 'A dog chasing a cat'. The caller points to one of the players nearby who has to walk past the catcher acting the part. The caller continues to call out different characters or animals until all the players have had a turn. The catcher then removes the blindfold. The caller names one of the characters and the catcher tries to guess who played the part. The catcher is allowed three guesses. If they guess correctly, they change places with that child who then becomes the catcher. If their guess is not correct after three attempts, they play the catcher for a second time. The caller also changes places with another player after each round.

---

2   Dunn, O. (1978) *Let's Play Asian Children's Games*. Macmillan Southeast Asia in association with the Asian Cultural Centre for UNESCO, pp.59–61.

Adaptations

- Think up a list of possible characters before starting the game.
- Use appropriate props (such as a walking stick) to increase the complexity of the characteristics that the catcher is listening out for.
- Use different emotions, such as 'walk happily'. The catcher guesses the emotion and/or the player.

Talk about

Was it easy or difficult to recognize the players? Why was this? What sort of things were you listening for to help you to identify the players?

Players need to use their imaginations to think about being different characters. Why is this an important ability?

What image did listeners have in their imagination for each character?

As you couldn't see the person, you had to make up an image. How easy or difficult was this?

How easy or difficult was it for players to change character?

How could this game help us to understand what it might be like to be someone else?

EXPANSION ACTIVITY 5.1. WHAT ARE IMAGES?

Ask each child to draw something that comes from their imagination.

Talk about

What are some of the differences and similarities between all the pictures? (I suggest that you model this to start with to minimize the possibility of children commenting on accuracy or style of drawing. If any children choose not to share their pictures with the group that is okay too. Talk about all the different types of possible images. For example, some will be like pictures, some will be sounds (like imagining a conversation or a tune in your head), and some will be feeling or sensation images (like imagining the feel of velvet or mud, or imagining what it might be like for your friend to feel sad)).

Have you ever made up a story in your head? Imagined that you saw something that wasn't really there? Heard a noise and imagined that it was something scary? Have you ever remembered the taste or feel of something that isn't actually in front of you? Do you ever imagine that you are somewhere else or doing something different? These are all images and they come from your imagination.

We all have the power of imagination and we can all use our imagination to help ourselves to sort out problems, feel good, cope with troubles when they come along and to help us to do the things that we want to do. (See the accompanying eBook *Using Imagination, Mindful Play and Creative Thinking to Support Wellbeing and Resilience in Children* for further guidelines on using imagery.)

EXPANSION ACTIVITY 5.2. TALKING CATS

Complete activity sheet 5.2 together.

Talk about

If we do something regularly, we stop thinking about it too much after a while and just do it, but we can still imagine it or recall the pictures from our mind when we want to. In the same way, when something new is about to happen, we can imagine what it might be like. This can be very useful. We can also imagine things that may never happen at all. This can be useful too – it helps us to think creatively. Sometimes we might make up things that worry us and we begin to believe that they are true. How can we help ourselves to use our imagination wisely when a big change is about to happen?

EXPANSION ACTIVITY 5.3. BECOMING A CAT

Read activity sheet 5.3 together. This activity helps children to understand a little bit more about how we can construct images in our imagination and could lead on to a discussion about seeing events and people's actions and words from different perspectives (what we think we know about something or someone might not always be accurate). See 'Talk about' in 'Expansion activity 2.2. Is this how you see me?'

6. Show me how you feel

Wellbeing focus:

☑ Self-confidence   ☑ Self-awareness

Examples of personal skills learned or consolidated:

☑ Observation   ☑ Recognizing and understanding
☑ Taking turns/tolerating waiting   emotions
                                     ☑ Thinking independently

Examples of general/social learning:

☑ Development of body awareness   ☑ Understanding empathy
   and positive body image   ☑ Dramatic awareness

How to play

Each player picks an emotion card (pictures or words) from a provided set. Players stand in a circle and take turns to jump forward and show the chosen feelings (by physical posture and facial expression). The group tries to guess the emotion. Everyone then tries to copy what this looks like.[3]

Adaptation

• Have several cards for a limited number of emotions. If players pick an emotion that has already been shown by someone else, they try to show it in a different way.

Talk about

How do we recognize feelings in ourselves and in others? Why is it important for other people to know how we feel? When might it be okay to physically show our emotions? When might it not be okay (such as hitting someone when we are

---

3   Some psychologists make a distinction between *feelings* (such as feelings of wellbeing, thirst or pain) and *emotions* (such as anger or sadness). Since we don't tend to do this in our daily interactions, I have used the terms interchangeably in the relevant games and activities.

Copyright © Deborah M. Plummer – *Helping Children to Manage Transitions* – 2022

angry)? What are some of the different emotions that we might feel when we are about to make a big change?

How many different ways can you think of to show excitement? How many different ways can you show worry?

EXPANSION ACTIVITY 6.1. HOW I FEEL

Complete activity sheet 6.1 together. Children are often labelled according to their behaviour at an early age and may quickly absorb these labels into their belief systems about themselves. If a child has always been told 'You're so grumpy all the time', then that is what they will believe and they are likely to act accordingly. They will need to experience alternative, genuine feedback (such as 'I thought you were really happy and confident when you did that activity'). This will need to be frequent and from a number of different people in order for a child to start to change their self-concept. Talking about a range of feelings and how feelings can change will help in this respect.

Talk about

Choose a feeling and talk about children being in a similar situation but feeling something different. Compare all the different things that might lead to children feeling excited or nervous. Feelings can change – what we might once have been nervous about we might eventually come to enjoy or to feel more confident about.

Point out any feelings that are similar in the group ('It sounds as though most of us get excited when...' 'Almost everyone feels nervous when...' 'There are a few of us who feel disappointed when...').

EXPANSION ACTIVITY 6.2. MORE FEELINGS

Complete activity sheet 6.2 together.

Talk about

Reassure the children about the normality of feelings related to big changes. Share feelings about the first day of school, the first day at an after-school club, etc. (It may be appropriate to briefly share one of your own memories. It is important for children to know that adults can have similar feelings or that they may have had them when they were young too.) Explore suggestions as to what made it okay or what might have made it easier. What can we do to help ourselves in these situations? What can we ask other people to do?

Skills and Resources

By doing the activities in this section you will be helping children to:

- understand that change is a natural part of life
- identify some of their worries and concerns about change
- identify strengths and resources
- understand that they can build skills to cope with change successfully.

7. All change

Wellbeing focus:

☑ Self-confidence   ☑ Self-awareness

Examples of personal skills learned or consolidated:

☑ Memory strategies   ☑ Observation
☑ Waiting   ☑ Focusing attention

Examples of general/social learning:

☑ Awareness of others   ☑ Awareness that 'change' can
                                                    happen in varying degrees

How to play
One player leaves the room. Someone in the group changes something about themselves (such as removing one shoe, putting on a jumper, or something more subtle, such as tying back their hair). The observer returns and tries to guess who has changed and what they have changed.

Adaptation

• Two players leave the room. Three people change something physically or change places and the two players have to say what the changes are.

Talk about
What has changed and what has stayed the same? Were these big changes or small changes?
      Think of a time when a small change might lead to a much bigger change.
      Even when there is a big change to cope with, there will still be lots of parts of the situation or the people involved that will stay the same. Can you think of a time when you have experienced this?

EXPANSION ACTIVITY 7.1. I SPY

Play an 'I spy' game or set an 'I spy' task where children look for changes in their environment that might have happened recently. There might be natural changes such as trees losing their leaves, plants coming into flower or a newly built bird's nest. Changes that have been made by people might be such things as a new display of pictures in a classroom or a new piece of play equipment in the local playground.

Point out aspects of personal change linked with the children's observations. 'Do you remember the time when…that was fun wasn't it?' Or 'You noticed lots of changes in the park. When you moved to a new class there were lots of changes too – that was a bit hard to start with wasn't it? It was good that we could all help each other.'

Talk about observation skills and looking with full awareness as opposed to just 'glancing' at something. Why do we need to be selective in what we pay attention to at any one time?

EXPANSION ACTIVITY 7.2. EXPERIMENTS

Experiment with small changes. For example, everyone tastes a new food that they've never tried before or plays a new game together. Then everyone changes one thing that they usually do without thinking about it (a habit). What does this feel like? As an example, if a child is right-handed, can they hold their bottle of water in their left hand? Can the children sit in a different position while they are reading or while they are waiting their turn in a game?

Talk about

For how long can you remember to do this? How easy or difficult is it to make these two sorts of changes? Are there any benefits? What type of change is involved in changing how we think about something? Would we be changing a habit, or trying something new, or both? What might be hard about changing our thoughts? What might be easy? See the following activity, '8. The worry box'.

8. The worry box

Wellbeing focus:

- ☑ Self-confidence
- ☑ Self-awareness

Examples of personal skills learned or consolidated:

- ☑ Sharing feelings and concerns
- ☑ Planning
- ☑ Making choices

Examples of general/social learning:

- ☑ Building trust
- ☑ Building self-respect and respect for others

Make a brightly coloured 'worry box' and invite the children to post any worries that they might have about a particular change. Set aside a time, as often as you feel is necessary, to check the worry box together and to 'problem-solve' any worries that are there.

Remind the children that they don't need to think about the worries once they have written them down because they will be looked at during the designated time. If a child is particularly anxious you may find that you need a worry-checking time more often to start with, and that the same or similar worries might be repeated.

The worry box was always well used in our therapy groups. Because the worries will be read out it is, of course, important to tell the children beforehand that these will be discussed in the group (although they can be posted anonymously). I know that some schools already use this idea, and one of the things to be aware of is that teachers or therapists may find some worries posted that would need to be taken further because they potentially involve others. In our groups, worries centred quite naturally on speech and language difficulties and feelings of anxiety when speaking. There was once a worry about nightmares posted and the group came up with some excellent suggestions for dealing with this. Once the worry has been resolved, or the child feels that they are coping with it, then the piece of paper can be ceremoniously torn up or put through the shredder.

Children may have some suggestions about what they would like to happen with regard to their own worries. Some of these may not be realistic, but you can acknowledge the wish behind it. Then explore what else would help them to feel in control of worry thoughts. Make your own suggestions too, but be prepared for the children to reject these if they don't feel quite right!

Encourage the children to think of lots of different solutions with you and to pick their own strategies from a selection. This can be far more effective than telling a child just one way of dealing with a worry.

Craig (aged seven) was having a tough time at school because he was finding 'everything too hard'. He began to cry every morning and to plead with his mother to keep him at home. Craig wrote an 'I hate school because' list outlining all his worries. He made two versions – one for him to talk about with his mother and one to go in the worry box – with each worry on a separate slip of paper. In fact, unasked, Craig re-wrote his list at home and decorated it. His mother took it to school and discussed the contents with the headteacher. Within days the worries had been mostly addressed and Craig had stopped crying in the mornings. On his next visit to see me he asked if we could tear up all the worries except one that hadn't been 'fixed' yet!

Talk about

Do you think everyone has worries? Do people worry about the same sorts of things? Are some worries useful? What happens when worries take up a lot of thinking time and aren't resolved?

Writing a worry down or telling someone else often helps to make it seem less troublesome.

When you are worried is it the whole of you that feels worried or just a part of you?

Who do you share your worries with? Can you think of someone who could be your 'worry buddy'?

Note: To encourage an element of choice, children can be given the option to complete either or both of the next two expansion activities, or you could combine the two discussions and then give children the choice of which activity sheet to complete.

EXPANSION ACTIVITY 8.1. ANY MORE WORRIES?

Facilitate a discussion about what could happen to worries that are posted in a worry box.

Encourage fantasy solutions as well as more practical ones. For example: 'They should be tied up in a bundle and sent to _____ who would read each one and discuss them with _____.' 'Laws would be passed to make _____ illegal.' 'Everyone who had ever worried about _____ would receive _____.' 'All the worries would then be _____.'

Complete activity sheet 8.1 together.

EXPANSION ACTIVITY 8.2. THE WORRY TEAM

Facilitate a discussion about what could happen to worries (see activity sheet 8.2).

What would you like your worries to do? Imagine this happening. What happens next? Then what happens? For example, worries can disappear, grow bigger, shrink or change into something else. We could make friends with them, throw them away, send them to the moon, or take them to 'obedience' classes!

EXPANSION ACTIVITY 8.3. CATCHING WORRY THOUGHTS

Read activity sheet 8.3 together. Take turns to think up ideas about what to do with the worry thought in the net.

EXPANSION ACTIVITY 8.4. MAKE A PLAN

Outline different situations and talk about what children might specifically do, using ideas from all the activity sheets completed. Making a plan will help children to feel more in control of their worries. Encourage them to think of at least three things that they can do for each situation. For example: 'When I notice myself getting uptight/having a worry thought I will…'

9. The resilience tree

Wellbeing focus:

☑ Self-confidence   ☑ Self-awareness

Examples of personal skills learned or consolidated:

☑ Understanding metaphors   ☑ Understanding similarities
☑ Understanding characteristics

Examples of general/social learning:

☑ Building trust   ☑ Building self-respect and respect
                                       for others

As part of this imagery the children first discuss the meaning of resilience and the concept of resources for resilience. They then use their own name for a 'tree of resilience' (for example, the 'hardy tree' or the 'strong tree' or the 'helps me tree'). Once you have a name for the tree, invite the children to sit quietly on their chairs or on the floor or on top of a parachute ready to stretch their imagination. This imagery is a lovely one to do outside in a green space too, and you can add some movement and stretching as well so that children 'embody' the feeling of resilience. You could then finish by inviting the children to draw the tree or make a collage or an outdoor picture on the ground made from natural materials.

I suggest that you join the children in this imaginary journey so that you can get a feel for the timing of the questions and when it might feel right to move on. Children are usually very quick to say what they can see and feel, but if there is continued reticence you might also want to contribute your own experiences – 'As this tree I can see a long way across the field. Does anyone else want to say what they can see?' (There are further guidance notes for using imagery in *Using Imagination, Mindful Play and Creative Thinking to Support Wellbeing and Resilience in Children*.)

Read the following with plenty of pauses so that the children can take time to explore the images.

The resilience tree

Settle yourself into a comfortable position and allow your eyes to close... Allow your imagination to take you to a special mountain... Imagine that you are standing in a field at the bottom of this mountain ready to go on a walk... [Wait a moment for the children to begin to get an image.] In front of you there is a gate. Walk slowly towards it... It's a very special gate. Can you see what it is made of?... Is there anything growing around it?... What does it feel like when you touch it?... Would anyone like to tell us about their gate?... When you are ready, imagine yourself going through the gate and standing on the other side.

Close the gate carefully behind you. You are standing on a path... Listen carefully, what can you hear on the mountain? [Invite the children to tell you what they can hear.] You are going to look for the [resilience] tree. It is near the gate somewhere. Have a look around at all the trees until you see the biggest one. This is the [resilience] tree... Give me a thumbs up when you have found the tree... Everyone has found the tree [or, if any children don't raise their hand or give a thumbs up sign: 'It's okay if you can't see the tree yet, it will soon come into your imagination']. Now imagine that you are standing right up against the tree. Touch the bark... What does it feel like? Does anyone want to say what the bark of the tree feels like? Look up into the branches of the tree. What can you see?...

What do you think it would feel like to *be* this tree? Imagine being this tree for a little while... [If appropriate, ask the children to stand up or sit very upright and imagine themselves as their tree.] What does that feel like?... What can you see?... What can you hear?... How do your branches move?... What sounds do you make when you move?... What do you most like about being this tree? What are the good feelings that you have as this tree?... When you are ready, imagine going back to being you again, standing next to the tree... What would you like to say to the tree?

Be very still for a moment and notice how you are feeling now... It's time to leave the mountain for today. Go through the gate and close it again behind you... step into the field.

Now the images start to fade...start to think about your toes and your fingers. Give them a little wriggle... Keep your eyes closed and feel how your body is gradually back in the room where you started. Notice the feel of your clothes against your skin and your body touching the chair... Still keep your eyes closed for a little while longer. Begin to listen to the sounds in the room and outside... Now wriggle your toes and fingers again and when you're ready have a big stretch and a yawn and open your eyes... And here you are back in the room!

Talk about

Our thoughts can affect how we feel and what we do. When we change our thoughts we can begin to feel differently too. If we remember that we have lots of skills to help us when we face change, or if we think about feeling as resilient as a resilience tree, that can help us to feel more confident about managing a change.

If your resilience tree could talk, what advice would it give you?

EXPANSION ACTIVITY 9.1. A VERY SPECIAL TREE

The aim in this activity is to help each child to identify people who will help and support them at times of change. It can also be used to help them to think more about available personal external and inner resources for building resilience. To begin with, I suggest limiting the number of connections to just four or five, particularly if you are working with a group. It is important that children are steered away from any possible negative evaluation of their tree in comparison to other group members (such as 'She has more friends than me', 'I only have one person who helps me').

How to play

Invite the children to draw a very special tree to show connections with family, friends and mentors. Each child draws a tree shape and puts their own name or their photo or a 'self-portrait' on one of the branches and the names or photos of 'important' people on some or all of the other branches. Spend time colouring and decorating the trees, making them unique.

Display the trees on the wall.

Adaptations

- Instead of drawing trees, the children draw around their own hand and write the names of important people on each finger. This is their 'hand of friendship' or their 'helping hand' (people who are close to them and who will help them if they get stuck).
- Make or draw a tree to hang 'resource' parcels on. These could be parcels showing or containing pictures relevant to both internal and

external resources such as a photo or drawing of a supporting adult or friend, a picture of a pet, a representation of what a child likes to do to relax. As you do more of the activities in this book you might steer children toward identifying more resources. Parcels can be added whenever a new resource is identified or 'unwrapped' when needed for an upcoming change.

Talk about

Who or what is on each tree? What *sort* of tree have you drawn? Is it an apple tree, a willow tree, a very ancient tree, a magic tree? (It is not necessary to interpret any of the drawings, but do encourage older children to elaborate on the characteristics of their tree – strong, protective, new, wild, orderly, etc.) What are the similarities and differences between your tree and the other children's trees?

Think about the differences and similarities between support from others and 'inner' support. What strengths and skills do you have to help you to manage little changes and big changes?

EXPANSION ACTIVITY 9.2. IMPORTANT PEOPLE

Complete activity sheet 9.2 together. This can be extended to discussing and drawing important events, places and objects. Identifying important aspects of their life helps children to recognize internal and external resources. What 'gift' have these important people, places and events given to the children that will help them to manage changes now and in the future? For example, an important place might be somewhere that they could go, or could imagine themselves being, when they need to re-energize or calm themselves. Perhaps an important person has some wise advice about coping with change or has coped with a recent change themselves and can share the experience. An important person might simply be someone who 'understands' (see 'Expansion activity 10.1. My display cabinet').

10. Skill mix

Wellbeing focus:

☑ Self-confidence   ☑ Self-awareness

Examples of personal skills learned or consolidated:

☑ Cooperation   ☑ Problem-solving
☑ Observation

Examples of general/social learning:

☑ Exploring self-concept and   ☑ Developing sensitivity to
self-efficacy   other people's strengths and
                                     differences

This game needs some preparation beforehand. You will need to find or draw a large picture of a building such as a castle. Paste this onto card and then cut the picture into enough puzzle pieces to provide one piece for each player in the group.

How to play

Players identify one skill that they already have or are currently developing. They draw something to represent this skill on the back of a puzzle piece. When all the players have completed a drawing, the group tries to make the puzzle in a given time limit. This can be done by using the original picture of a building or by shape alone. Tape the pieces together so that either side of the finished puzzle can be displayed.

Adaptations

- Use a picture to represent resilience (such as a superhero or an oak tree). Make puzzle pieces to show external resources, or a mixture of skills and external resources, that will help the children to manage transitions.

- Use large plastic bricks or bricks drawn on card to build a structure (wall, house, school, etc.) with different skills on each brick or different things of which players are proud.

Talk about

Discuss learning 'sets' of skills and how we build up abilities gradually. Compare this to having a natural ability that can be practised and developed (such as singing). Are there some skills that everyone needs? How might members of the group share their expertise with others? How might it be useful for different group members to have different skills?

Think about the internal resources needed for wellbeing.

EXPANSION ACTIVITY 10.1. MY DISPLAY CABINET

Invite the children to draw pictures or write in their personal display cabinet to show some of their personal skills (see activity sheet 10.1).

Adaptation

- The children draw things that are important to them (such as an important person, a special fact, favourite food, an important day, the thing they hate the most). Younger children could choose something that they have with them or something they are wearing that they particularly like or that is important to them. They can talk about this in turn or draw the object in their display cabinet.

Talk about

There are many different types of things that can have a special meaning for us. During times of change many of these special things will stay the same. Sometimes change brings new special things – new skills, new special friends and so on.

EXPANSION ACTIVITY 10.2. THE MAGIC MIRROR

The children draw self-portraits in the magic mirror or fill the mirror with words and pictures representing each child's strengths and skills (see activity sheet 10.2). The mirror can be used at different stages of a major change too. For example, the children could draw themselves or draw pictures of how things will be when the change has taken place (see '19. Imagine making a change' and '25. Spaceship to the stars').

EXPANSION ACTIVITY 10.3. APPRECIATION

Complete activity sheet 10.3 together. Encourage the children to make personal 'asset jigsaws' and to add to these over time.

Thinking about Change

By doing the activities in this section you will be helping children to:

- further develop the ability to recognize and monitor the links between feelings and thoughts
- develop or consolidate skills for coping with the unexpected
- think about different types of change.

11. Word play

Wellbeing focus:

- ☑ Self-awareness
- ☑ Self-confidence

Examples of personal skills learned or consolidated:

- ☑ Listening
- ☑ Taking turns
- ☑ Cooperation

Examples of general/social learning:

- ☑ Building trust
- ☑ Understanding empathy
- ☑ Building self-respect and respect for others
- ☑ Dramatic awareness
- ☑ Developing sensitivity to other people's strengths and differences
- ☑ Exploring links between thoughts, feelings and actions

You will need four or five pieces of card with either a picture showing a change of some sort and/or a brief description such as 'Break time will be shorter today' or 'Sam is going to get a new puppy'.

How to play

The children collaborate in two groups to make a list of as many words or phrases as they can think of to do with change. For example:

scary, exciting, worrying, interesting, challenging, funny, sad, quick, slow, controlled, uncontrolled, made by me, made by someone else, stressful, puzzling, good, horrible

Each group then chooses three of their words or phrases that they will act in front of the other group. They then take one of the cards and have just two minutes to decide how they will demonstrate the change in the three ways they have chosen. For example, they could all show the same actions or emotions at the same time and do three in a row, or different children could act out different emotions while one child demonstrates the scenario.

Adaptations

- Discuss the various card prompts before the children choose one.
- Have just one scenario in mind. Briefly discuss this before the children come up with their list of words.
- The children act out a scenario where all three actions or emotions change during the chosen event. In this instance you could add extra time for the groups to devise a short play and to rehearse it. You might want to set a time limit or build in the option of groups negotiating a time to complete their scenario.

Talk about

Allow the children time to explore all the possible feelings and to feel reassured that it is normal to be worried or scared about some changes and excited about others.

Group discussions can result in more ideas and different observations than when we work on our own. How might this help us when we are facing a big change?

Different people can experience the same or similar event in different ways. This leads on to the next activity.

12. Different ways of thinking

Wellbeing focus:

- ☑ Self-awareness
- ☑ Self-confidence

Examples of personal skills learned or consolidated:

- ☑ Thinking independently
- ☑ Taking turns
- ☑ Concentration

Examples of general/social learning:

- ☑ Building trust
- ☑ Understanding empathy
- ☑ Building self-respect and respect for others
- ☑ Developing sensitivity to other people's strengths and differences
- ☑ Exploring links between thoughts, feelings and actions

How to play

Give each child a blank piece of paper and a pencil and tell them that they have five minutes to do something creative with these materials. Assure them that they do not have to finish whatever they decide on – they can just make a start. When you are ready, share the ideas. Have a group discussion about what a pencil and paper could be used for. How many different things can the group come up with? When you have twenty, think of five more – the last few are likely to be the most innovative!

Talk about

Three people who are all given a piece of blank paper and a pencil but no instructions as to what to do with them will probably have very different feelings about it. For example – panic ('I don't know what to do', 'I'm no good at deciding', 'I can't think up good ideas', 'I know that whatever I do will be wrong'); enthu-siasm ('I can do anything that I want', 'I've got loads of good ideas', 'I love the freedom of experimenting'); or anxiety expressed as anger ('How am I expected to know what she wants?', 'What does she think I am – a mind-reader?', 'She just wants to keep me quiet for a while', 'This is really boring'). Do you think different people see big and little changes in different ways too? Why do you think that?

Different people might also notice the same event in different ways. Two people seeing a fight in the playground will remember different details depending on where they were standing and perhaps their alliances with the people involved. Events have significance in themselves, but more important, perhaps, is the way in which we interpret them. This determines our consequent actions and our view of ourselves.

What one person thinks is stressful, another may see as fun or as an exciting challenge. One perception is not better or 'more right' than another – they are just different ways of looking at things (see 'Expansion activity 2.2. Is this how you see me?'). Sometimes our thoughts become automatic. Automatic thoughts can sometimes be useful – they can save us thinking time! But if they are unhelpful thoughts, then we can learn to recognize these and can begin to take control of them.

EXPANSION ACTIVITY 12.1. JUNK THOUGHTS

Complete activity sheet 12.1 together.

Talk about

'Junk thoughts' can be explained in terms of eating healthy food and 'junk' food. When we think thoughts like 'I'm hopeless' or 'I can't do this' or 'No one will speak to me', this is like eating junk food. These thoughts affect us in an unhelpful way. When we have thoughts like 'I can learn how to do this', 'This might be difficult but I'm going to have a go', 'It's okay if I make a mistake while I'm still learning' or 'I know how to be a good friend', then this is like eating healthy food and these thoughts are good for us.

13. Good news and bad news

Wellbeing focus:

☑ Self-confidence   ☑ Self-awareness

Examples of skills learned or consolidated:

☑ Understanding opposites   ☑ Sequencing/story-telling
☑ Understanding consequences   ☑ Taking turns

Examples of general/social learning:

☑ Flexibility of thought   ☑ Adaptability
☑ Coping with the unexpected

How to play
Players sit in a circle. The game coordinator starts off with a piece of 'good' news. The next person adds 'but the bad news is…' For example: 'The good news is that it will be sunny all morning… The bad news is that there is a storm coming.' 'The good news is that it's only a small storm… The bad news is that I forgot to bring my rain jacket.' 'The good news is that I have an umbrella… The bad news is that it's broken.'

Adaptations

- Make the story adventurous, amazing, scary or ridiculous!
- Play this in pairs with a strict time limit.
- Players throw a soft ball or bean bag to another player who will say the next sentence.

Talk about
For this game, you were being creative in thinking up ways to link the good news and the bad news. Was it easier to think up good news or bad news? Why is that? Have you ever been in a difficult situation that turned out to be useful for you? Can you remember how the story started off?

14. Story challenge

Wellbeing focus:

☑ Self-awareness   ☑ Self-confidence

Examples of personal skills learned or consolidated:

☑ Cooperation   ☑ Understanding and using non-
☑ Memory strategies   verbal communication

Examples of general/social learning:

☑ Coping with the unexpected   ☑ Developing sensitivity to
☑ Building trust   other people's strengths and
☑ Exploring links between   differences
   thoughts, feelings and actions   ☑ Adaptability
                                    ☑ Dramatic awareness

This game takes coping with the unexpected to a whole new level! This is a complex game suitable for older and more able children, although it can be simplified by removing the dialogue element. It is important that the players don't know what sequences have been given to other teams.

How to play
Divide the group into smaller teams of three to four players. Each team is given a short non-verbal sequence to practise, such as putting up a tent, hanging out the washing on a very windy day, or catching a dog and giving it a bath. One team silently demonstrates their sequence to the rest of the group. A second team is then chosen to repeat what they have just seen and add their own dialogue. Continue until all teams have acted their own sequence and put a dialogue to another team's sequence.

Adaptation

- Groups are told that they are going to tell a story using objects collected from outside or from the room (one object for each person). They are given ten minutes to collect their objects and to think of a theme for their story. Instead of telling their own story, however, each group then swaps their objects with another group who tells an unrehearsed story with each person taking an equal part.

Talk about

What might be helpful about working in a group when something unexpected comes along? What might make this easier? What might make it harder?

EXPANSION ACTIVITY 14.1. CHOICES

Each child thinks of a change that they have made or would like to make because they want to (such as choosing a new family pet or changing their bedroom) and one change that has happened that they had no, or little, choice about (such as a friend moving away).

Talk about

What are some of the differences and similarities between the two types of change? Why would someone choose to make a change? (Perhaps because they want to feel better, because someone else suggests it, because they think they should, because they want to be like their friends?) What do we need to have or to know in order to make a successful change? (We might need to know what the change will involve, we may need help from others, we might need to really want the change to work for us.)

What makes change easier to cope with? (Perhaps when there are lots of people making the same change, when we have already made a similar change so we can guess what it is going to be like, when we can talk to someone about it, if we can meet someone from the new place, if we can visit a new place to have a look around?) What can we do to keep feeling okay about the change? (Reward ourselves, continue to set small goals.)

15. Our change story

Wellbeing focus:

☑ Self-confidence   ☑ Self-awareness

Examples of personal skills learned or consolidated:

☑ Shifting attention   ☑ Concentration
☑ Self-control   ☑ Waiting
☑ Listening

Examples of general/social learning:

☑ Reducing impulsivity   ☑ Awareness of others

This is a variation of a popular game called 'The old family coach'.

How to play

The game coordinator makes up a short story about the group, based around a time of change and using each player's name at least three times. When a player hears their own name they stand up, turn round three times and take a bow! When the game coordinator says 'all the children' or 'everyone' the whole group stands up, turns round three times and takes a bow.

For example: 'The new classroom was ready at last and *all the children* waited excitedly in the playground on the first day of term. The headteacher asked *Edward* and *Jodie* to fetch the registers from the office. On the way inside they bumped into *Karen* and *Amarjeet* who had gone to fetch the school bell. *Sam* was allowed to ring the bell and he rang it so loudly that *Marcus* and *Sandeep* put their hands over their ears. Then *Edward* and *Michèle* led everyone into their new classroom...'

Adaptations

- Make the story complex, exciting or scary, so that players need to swap between being absorbed in the story and listening for their names.
- Use a response that requires only slight or no physical movement.

- Use musical instruments for players to signal when they hear their name.
- Base the story on an imaginary situation where things went wrong because no one was listening and the children had to put everything right.

Talk about

What do you feel if you don't hear something important? Is it easy or difficult to focus on one thing (for example, names) when you are listening to a story? Why is this?

Is it usually easy or difficult for you to hear instructions when you are trying to solve a problem? Why is this? What would make this game easier? What would make it harder?

How might careful listening help us in times of change? What sorts of changes are fun?

EXPANSION ACTIVITY 15.1. STORY-TELLING

Change, personal growth and overcoming adversity are, of course, central themes for children's novels and picture books, so there are many to choose from for all ages. I have some old favourites, but there are so many good quality children's books that you will very quickly find your own preferred selection. A personalized story or one that children have helped to devise is also well worth the initial time taken in preparation (see the guidelines for wellbeing stories in the accompanying eBook *Using Imagination, Mindful Play and Creative Thinking to Support Wellbeing and Resilience in Children*). If you are already a keen story-teller, then I would certainly weave stories into as many of your IMPACT sessions with children as possible. If you are just starting off, then please be assured that children love listening to stories so much that I'm sure you will want to tell more and more!

Most children like to have a routine to their days and will feel more secure and less stressed if they can predict what might happen. You might want to emphasize this aspect in a story, noting things that stay the same and how small changes that are part of a bigger change can be managed in steps (see the games and activities in section V).

- Make up a story together about how a child or animal has coped with change.

- Tell a familiar story of how someone in the past has coped with adversity (such as someone famous or a grandparent or other family member).
- Retell events related to an actual future or past change but 'storify' it by making the child protagonist into a superhero or familiar character from their play experiences.
- Tell the story of a sporting hero who, against all odds, went from playing alone to joining a team.

EXPANSION ACTIVITY 15.2. THE BOOK OF WISDOM

Read activity sheet 15.2 together.

I'm sure that most of us have had the experience of coming up with a solution to a difficult problem when we were least expecting it. We think about it for hours and come to no conclusions, so we give up and go for a walk, and suddenly the answer seems crystal clear! Or perhaps you have tried to think of a name or a song title but couldn't remember it, and then suddenly there it is – just as you are falling asleep that night. Once again, naming the problem or defining the question can help to take some of the worry out of it. Inevitably the child's innate wisdom will help them to sort it, even if that wisdom tells them to ask someone for help.

16. Tell me my story

Wellbeing focus:

☑ Self-confidence   ☑ Self-awareness

Examples of skills learned or consolidated:

☑ Listening   ☑ Taking turns
☑ Sequencing/story-telling   ☑ Maintaining a topic

Examples of general/social learning:

☑ Building trust
☑ Understanding empathy
☑ Building self-respect and respect for others

☑ Developing sensitivity to other people's strengths and differences

How to play

The game coordinator provides a title that includes a child's name, such as:

Marcus the bold

Amazing Craig

Javed's dream day out

Katie's greatest adventure

The player in question starts off the story. The rest of the group continues around the circle, saying one sentence each. This could be a completely imaginary story about coping with a big change, or it could relate to something that everyone knows really happened.

Adaptations

- Youngsters love to hear and tell stories about themselves, and it is really worth spending time retelling these. For example, 'Yesterday Josh told us this story about when he first came to live in this town... On the first morning Josh and his mum were in the park and...'

- Take turns to tell the story of important transitions such as 'The day I started school', 'When I lost my front teeth' or 'When we moved to a new house'. In a group, providing a theme that you know is familiar to most or all of the group is a good way to help children to explore similarities and differences in how we each cope with situations. It is also very affirming for individual children. Alternatively, if you think it advisable in a particular group, invite each child to talk about a completely different event. This will minimize the chance of children making unfavourable comparisons in relation to how the same events are negotiated by individuals.
- Have a selection of three or four titles written up so each child can choose their own title.
- Encourage the children to think up their own title for their story.

Talk about
Was this difficult, exciting, funny or easy? Did the group come up with some things that truly reflected your personality and skills? How did it feel to listen to a story about yourself? Did you hear anything in the stories about other people that might be helpful for you?

Making a Change

By doing the activities in this section you will be helping children to:

- understand the need to prepare for big changes and challenges
- continue to think about unexpected aspects of change
- identify useful problem-solving skills
- recognize successes
- recognize how some changes can be managed in small steps.

17. Finger carry

Wellbeing focus:

☑ Self-confidence   ☑ Self-awareness

Examples of personal skills learned or consolidated:

☑ Problem-solving   ☑ Tolerating frustration
☑ Cooperation

Examples of general/social learning:

☑ Learning the social value of individual skills and achievements   ☑ Understanding the concepts of joint responsibility and encouraging others

How to play

Small groups of players (four to six per group) are given a set of small objects of various shapes and weights that they must transport from one side of the room to the other. Each player can only use one finger of one hand and must keep the other hand behind their back. The aim is to move the objects within a set time limit (which is decided according to the dexterity of the players and the number of objects being used).

Adaptation

- If an object is dropped the players start from the beginning again.

Talk about

What do you feel when you solve a problem either individually or as a group? What skills are involved in problem-solving?

Do you feel comfortable asking for help when something is difficult? Think of a time when you have helped someone else. How did that feel? How did the other person respond? Has anyone ever helped you out when you didn't need or want their help? How does that feel? What could you say in that situation? (For example, 'Thank you for offering to help but I really want to do this for myself.')

When might you like help with managing a change? What sort of things would you not want help with?

EXPANSION ACTIVITY 17.1. INVOLVE

Within a time limit (ten minutes is usually long enough) the children work in pairs or groups to redesign a game that you have provided for them. For example, they might choose to simplify it or to make it more complex, or to change it from an active game to one that can be played sitting down. When the time is up they are then given a similar length of time to change any game of their own choosing. After comparing the different results, talk about any differences and similarities in the process itself. How did the children feel about choosing how to play a game that had been provided by someone else? How did they feel about choosing their own game and choosing how to play it? Sometimes we are not able to choose the changes in our lives but perhaps we can be involved in making decisions about part of the change, or we can choose how we are going to *manage* the change.

EXPANSION ACTIVITY 17.2. SIGNPOSTS

The children each draw a picture of a recent time when they have felt pleased with something that they have achieved in relation to a change. When everyone has drawn their picture, ask them to imagine that they can see a signpost nearby that shows them what this achievement led on to (or what it might lead to in the future). For example, 'I achieved my aim of practising calm breathing and that meant that I felt calmer when I went into my new class.' The signpost in this instance might read 'To Confidence', or could show a smiley face. Invite the children to add their signpost to their drawing. If they are not able to imagine what the signpost says, they can still add an unmarked sign – perhaps the direction will become more evident to them at a later time!

18. Guess what!

Wellbeing focus:

☑ Self-confidence   ☑ Self-awareness

Examples of personal skills learned or consolidated:

☑ Observation   ☑ Thinking independently

Examples of general/social learning:

☑ Flexibility of thought and action ☑ Dramatic awareness
☑ Coping with the unexpected

How to play

Provide a prop for the children to use in different ways. The rest of the group have to guess what it is (such as a small mat used as a wheelchair, a seat of a car, a shield, a cloak or rolled up as a sword).

You might want to think of a few ideas first or just let the children step forward as soon as they think of something.

Adaptation

• Provide two or three props that have to be combined together by pairs of children in a spontaneous and cooperative mime.

Talk about

It is often good to plan ahead, but sometimes we can over-plan things and get anxious about something long before it ever happens.

Sometimes the unexpected is even more fun or makes a change easier than we first thought it would be (see also 'Talk about' suggestions for '14. Story challenge').

19. Imagine making a change

We can help children to minimize the possible difficulties involved in change by giving them an opportunity to 'research' the risk in their imagination. This will enable them to get a sense of what the possible outcome and benefits might be when they have completed the intended change.

With appropriate adjustments for language level, the guidance for 'Exploratory activity 1.4. Imagining a change' can be used for children too. Encourage the children to imagine a positive outcome. This could be something like 'It is difficult, but I am coping well' or 'I have made a new friend'. Remind them that they are using their memory from the future, as if it had already happened, rather than just thinking about what it *might* be like. At the end of the exercise complete activity sheet 19 together. (See further guidance notes for using imagery with children in *Using Imagination, Mindful Play and Creative Thinking to Support Wellbeing and Resilience in Children*.)

Talk about

Imagining that you have already achieved a goal can sometimes be more powerful than planning what you will have to do beforehand. Athletes are often trained to see themselves having made the perfect high jump, having achieved their personal best time, and so on.

Our imagination can help us to cope with things successfully. If we imagine something clearly enough we create a memory – as if it had actually happened. The details may turn out to be quite different, but the feeling can be the same (such as confidence, excitement, etc.).

20. Pirate's treasure parachute game

Wellbeing focus:

☑ Self-confidence   ☑ Self-awareness

Examples of personal skills learned or consolidated:

☑ Listening   ☑ Memory strategies
☑ Cooperation

Examples of general/social learning:

☑ Building trust   ☑ Understanding empathy
☑ Building self-respect and respect   ☑ Exploring self-concept and
    for others   self-efficacy

This game offers an opportunity for children to review their personal resources and skills and to think about what they have been learning.

How to play
Players take turns to briefly describe an object that they have with them. This can be anything at all – a pencil, a jumper, a book and so on. Describing the item will help the children to remember who it belongs to. The 'treasures' are placed under a parachute. Players hold the parachute at waist level and make 'waves'. Divers take turns to go under the waves to gather one piece of treasure and return it to its owner. If they are unable to remember who the owner is, the coordinator gives clues that are related to generally known information about group members, such as 'This belongs to the person who doesn't like chocolate'.

Adaptations

- Retrieve treasure according to different qualities or shape, for example 'Find something wooden', 'Find something made of metal', 'Find something round'.
- Each child writes a personal skill on a piece of card, one that they are particularly proud of. Divers try to remember who these treasures belong

to. When they return them to their owners, they can congratulate them on owning such a great piece of treasure!

Talk about

Think about the skills and resources identified in earlier games and activities (see section III).

Our talents, abilities, personality characteristics and ideas are all examples of our personal 'treasure'. What new skills have you identified since the group started? How full is your treasure box?

Remind each other how these can help us to manage big changes.

21. I packed my backpack (or suitcase)

Wellbeing focus:

☑ Self-confidence ☑ Self-awareness

Examples of personal skills learned or consolidated:

☑ Listening ☑ Taking turns
☑ Memory strategies ☑ Categorizing

Examples of general/social learning:

☑ Understanding responsibility ☑ Exploring self-efficacy

This is a familiar memory game adapted to help children to think carefully about what they might need for different situations.

How to play

Think of a variety of different activities or adventures that would need different equipment and clothing as well as items that would be relevant for *any* situation (for example, mountaineering, deep sea diving, going to an adventure playground, visiting a hot country, visiting a cold country, going on a treasure hunt).

Choose one of these and play a round of 'I packed my backpack (or suitcase) and I took…' Each child has to remember what has already been packed and add one more item to the list. When the list gets too long to remember, choose another adventure and start again.

Anyone can challenge the inclusion of an item that doesn't seem relevant for the particular adventure.

Talk about

How can we prepare ourselves for adventures and challenges? If we think something is going to be scary, embarrassing or difficult, what could we do to help ourselves to cope with this?

EXPANSION ACTIVITY 21.1. PREPARE TO DIVE!

Complete activity sheet 21.1 together.

If a child was going to enter a sports competition or go on an arduous mountain trek, they would need to be properly prepared and would be supported and encouraged to take time to build their strength, skills and stamina beforehand. Yet how often are children faced with stressful situations in daily life feeling unprepared or unable to cope with the unknown? This activity can be used to discuss the importance of preparing for new or difficult things.

Talk about

What are research skills? On a scale of 1–5, where 1 is 'a little bit' and 5 is 'lots', how much do you enjoy researching things? How were you able to get to that level of enjoyment? (And/or 'What would help you to enjoy researching something even more?')

How can we research what we might need to know or have so that we feel prepared for changes?

22. Tangled up

Wellbeing focus:

☑ Self-confidence ☑ Self-awareness

Examples of personal skills learned or consolidated:

☑ Problem-solving ☑ Giving instructions
☑ Cooperation ☑ Observation

Examples of general/social learning:

☑ Understanding responsibility ☑ Understanding how individual
☑ Flexibility of thought and action   behaviour affects others

This is a well-known problem-solving game that children never seem to get tired of playing!

How to play
Two players leave the room. The rest of the group joins hands to form a chain. The person at one end begins to weave in and out, leading other members into a 'tangle' without breaking the links. Players can go over or under arms; between legs, etc. The two players return and try to untangle the group by giving instructions only. They cannot touch the chain at all.

Adaptations

- Players stand in a circle and then close their eyes and stretch out their hands to find other hands. They then open their eyes and try to untangle themselves without letting go.
- The 'problem-solvers' watch while the chain is becoming tangled.

Talk about
How did it feel to be the leader of the tangle? Did other members of the group join in with giving instructions?

How did it feel to be in the role of problem-solver? What were the important things to remember so that the chain did not break and no one got hurt?

Have you ever come across problems that seemed too complex to unravel at first? How could we tackle that sort of problem? Does this game involve a problem or a challenge?

It's okay to make mistakes or for things to not quite work out. By persevering and altering the way we approach the task or by improving our skills, we can often solve the problem.

How might the skills used in this game be helpful when we are making big changes?

EXPANSION ACTIVITY 22.1. SKILLS FOR PROBLEM-SOLVING

See activity sheet 22.1. Can you tie a knot in a piece of string without letting go of either end? The trick is to cross your arms before picking up the string!

Can you draw a dot inside a circle without taking your pen off the paper? Fold the corner of the page. Draw a dot at the tip of the folded corner. Draw a line towards the fold and then start to draw a circle across the fold. Open up the paper without taking your pen off and complete the circle.

23. Step up

Wellbeing focus:

☑ Self-confidence ☑ Self-awareness

Examples of personal skills learned or consolidated:

☑ Problem-solving ☑ Listening
☑ Cooperation

Examples of general/social learning:

☑ Building trust ☑ Understanding the concept of
☑ Flexibility of thought and action   inclusion

This game requires a large space and a supply of 'stepping-stones' made from paper or card.

How to play
Small groups of around six to eight players per group must cross a designated space by using a small number of stepping-stones (not enough to get them all the way across the space). No member of the group can touch the ground or floor. Five or six stones are normally enough for a group of eight.

Adaptations

- Groups use the stepping-stones to 'rescue' a player who is stranded on the other side of the space. The stranded player is blindfolded. If they come off a stepping-stone and touch any part of the floor, the rescue has to start from the beginning again.
- Create hazard zones to be avoided.

Talk about
Was there more than one way to solve the problem? How did group members cooperate? How did it feel to be the stranded player? Did you feel safe? What helped you to trust the group?

Steps towards a goal can be just a few, spread widely apart or many small steps. Changes can be made in stages or might happen in a rush. How might the skills used in this game help you to manage a particular change?

EXPANSION ACTIVITY 23.1. QUICK DRAW

Invite the children to draw the stages of one change that they have already coped with successfully. This could be a big change, such as moving to a new house, or a small change, such as starting to do regular exercise. Start with a picture of how things used to be. Draw a second picture that shows how things are now. Then draw a third picture showing how these changes happened.

Talk about

What were the steps that helped you to make the change? What did you need to know or have in order to make the change? What was the best bit about making the change? What was the worst bit? What are you most pleased about now that you have coped with the change?

Talk about the differences between big and small changes. What sorts of changes are scary? What sorts of changes are fun?

EXPANSION ACTIVITY 23.2. STEPS ALONG THE WAY

Use a diary, wall calendar or activity sheet 23.2 to mark the stages of preparation for a particular change. Colour in the steps as they are completed. Make sure that each step is well defined and is small enough to be manageable (but not too small so that you end up with too many steps or stages and risk a child losing motivation). (See also 'Exploratory activity 9.4. Taking steps' in the accompanying eBook *Using Imagination, Mindful Play and Creative Thinking to Support Wellbeing and Resilience in Children*.)

Taking Care of Myself

By doing the activities in this section you will be helping children to:

- reduce the effects of any stress involved in change
- learn some basic self-calming strategies.

24. Pass a smile

Wellbeing focus:

☑ Self-confidence   ☑ Self-awareness

Examples of skills learned or consolidated:

☑ Understanding opposites   ☑ Taking turns
☑ Observation   ☑ Recognizing and understanding
☑ Understanding and using non-   emotions
verbal communication

Examples of general/social learning:

☑ Flexibility of thought   ☑ Exploring links between
thoughts, feelings and actions

This is a fun group game, but can also be played with just two people.

How to play
Players sit in a circle. Everyone tries to look very serious. A child is chosen to start off a smile. They send a smile to the person sitting next to them. This person smiles, and then 'zips' their lips in order to 'hold' the smile. They then turn to the next person and unzip the smile to pass it on! When the smile has been around the circle once, the group have a go at passing another smile, but this time even more quickly.

Adaptations

- One player 'throws' a smile across the circle. Everyone has to stay on the alert to catch it!
- Players pass a frown or a look of surprise.
- Players alternate between two different expressions.

Talk about
How easy or difficult is it for you to control the expression on your face? Why is

this? It is sometimes possible to have control over how we feel. How does your body feel when you smile? What makes you smile? Can you tell the difference between a genuine smile and a pretend one or an 'unkind' smile? How can you tell the difference? Do you always know what expression you are showing on your face? For example, do you know when you are frowning or looking 'fed up'?

EXPANSION ACTIVITY 24.1. HUMOUR

Make up a nonsense song or a funny poem about change. Humour is a great stress buster and a boost to wellbeing.

Talk about
Sometimes laughing can help us to feel more relaxed. When might this be appropriate? When would it not be appropriate? Have you ever felt upset or worried about something that you could laugh about later? What makes you laugh? What makes your friend laugh?

EXPANSION ACTIVITY 24.2. WHEN I WANT TO CALM MYSELF

This is a useful self-calming strategy for children to learn. I also suggest that you teach children the mindful breathing activity that can be found in Appendix A of the accompanying eBook *Using Imagination, Mindful Play and Creative Thinking to Support Wellbeing and Resilience in Children*. There are many more ideas in *Helping Children to Manage Stress*.

> Gently close your eyes and feel yourself relaxing. When you breathe in you can feel a relaxing, warm feeling filling up your body. Each time you breathe out you are breathing away all the tightness in your muscles that you don't need. Feel the air as it very slowly goes in and out of you... Imagine that there is a yellow light that is coming up from beneath your feet. It moves through your feet...your legs...your body...your arms...your shoulders...and your head...and it goes through the top of your head and floats away...so now you feel very relaxed but still wide awake and ready to... [Move the children on to the next activity.]

EXPANSION ACTIVITY 24.3. TAKING CARE OF MYSELF EVERY DAY

Make a list together of 'Ways to look after myself' (see activity sheet 24.3). This can be very general or linked specifically to times of change. Try to think of at least 20 ideas. Help the children to choose up to three things that they will do when they are feeling worried, fed up or tired during the next week. Be specific. For example, 'When I notice myself getting up tight or upset I will... [go for a bike ride, relax on my bed, take some time for myself, play with the dog, talk to a friend, ask mum for a hug].'

Talk about

Can you think of some different things that children and adults can do to help themselves to feel relaxed? Have you ever needed to 'unwind' after you have been very busy?

(Encourage the children to think about emotional 'busyness' as well as physical 'busyness' and how physical activity can be one way to relax the mind.)

EXPANSION ACTIVITY 24.4. UNWIND

Do a relaxation session and record it so that the children can use this whenever they want to (thus taking control over their own relaxation on a regular basis). If you don't already have a favourite children's relaxation activity, there are several suggestions in *Helping Children to Manage Stress*.

VII

Reflecting on Change and Setting Goals

By doing the activities in this section you will be helping children to:

- explore the idea of setting regular goals
- develop strategies for monitoring their own progress
- celebrate achievements in coping with change
- appreciate members of the group and bring the group to a close.

Ups and downs are a natural part of any change. The children might continue to have days when they still feel confused or anxious despite their own efforts and those of supporting adults. It will be important to acknowledge these feelings before they grow out of proportion. Remind them that these difficult feelings will pass and that it is okay to miss something or talk about how things used to be. This doesn't mean that they can't enjoy something new.

25. Spaceship to the stars

This activity is adapted from original ImageWork exercises by Dr Dina Glouberman.[1] Projecting yourself into the future to imagine how things will turn out is a powerful aid to making changes. Such imagery requires the suspending of judgement and reality in order to act 'as if' you had already achieved your desired outcome.

It will be most effective if the children have a particular goal in mind before starting. As an alternative to a spaceship they could imagine going to their own private cinema, for example.

Find a comfortable position...and gently let your eyes close. Take three full breaths, breathing in right down into the bottom of your lungs and breathing out slowly and calmly.

Let's imagine that you can travel into the future in your own special spaceship. Imagine what that spaceship looks like... What colour is it?... What shape?

Notice what it sounds like. Can you see the spaceship door?... If you go inside you will see a really comfortable chair to sit in with some controls in front of it and a large window that goes half way around the ship.

Imagine yourself sitting at the controls. There are lots of them. There's a button that has a sign under it saying 'To the stars' and one that says 'Back home'. When you're ready to go all you have to do is press the button for the stars and the spaceship will gently take off and head up into the sky. You will be totally in control. Ready?... You're climbing high up into the sky...

You are travelling through the clouds. The sky around you is becoming a deeper and deeper blue and you can see the stars shining ahead of you.

Somewhere up here is your own special star...search around for a little while until you can see it really well... Notice all the little details about this very special star as the spaceship hovers near it and circles around it... If there is something you have to get done or a goal you want to set for yourself then this star will be able to show you what it will be like for you once you've achieved it.

Imagine that there is a beam of light shining out from your star into the sky. As you watch you can see a big screen forming in the sky ahead of you. Onto this screen walks a person...it's you! This is you after you've achieved your goal. [If you are working with one child and you know what their goal is, it would be helpful

1   Glouberman, D. (2003) *Life Choices, Life Changes*. London: Hodder & Stoughton.

to name it at this point. For example, 'You've finished your maths test', 'You've learned how to swim', 'You can ride your new bike', 'You've finished making that model and it's right there beside you'.]

What do you look like on the screen?... What is the 'future you' doing?... What did you do to make this happen?... What did you need to have or to know so that you could achieve your goal?... How is 'you' on the screen different from 'you' sitting in the spaceship?... If the 'future you' could whisper something special to 'you' in the spaceship, what would they whisper?... The 'future you' says goodbye and is walking away now. As you watch, the beam of light from the star begins to get fainter and the screen starts to fade until eventually it has disappeared...

If you like, you've got plenty of time just to play up here in the stars. You can make your spaceship go wherever you want. See what you can find up here! [Allow time for children to explore in silence.]

Time now to leave the stars. Take one last look around... Press the button that says 'Back home' and away goes the spaceship, through the deep blue sky... through the floating clouds...slowly and gently back down to the ground...

As you get out of the spaceship notice if you feel any different now to how you felt when you first set off... Now you're walking away from the spaceship. Feel yourself coming back to the room... Notice the feel of your body... Listen to the sounds around you... Keep your eyes closed for a little while longer while you have a little stretch... When you are ready, open your eyes and look around you... Stamp your feet on the floor a bit to bring you properly back down to earth!

Talk about

Think of all the different types of targets or goals that people can set for themselves at school, with friends, in sport, in the Scouts or Guides, etc. Think about individual targets and also group aims or goals. How do you feel when you have achieved a goal? What do other people notice about you when you are feeling good about achieving something? Thinking about the change(s) happening now or in the future, what goals do you have? How will you know when you have achieved these?

EXPANSION ACTIVITY 25.1. FUTURE ME

Invite the children to write a letter from the future, telling themselves how they achieved their goals, or giving themselves some advice about what to do if they notice themselves being worried about upcoming changes (see activity sheet 25.1). If appropriate for the group that you are running, you may want to provide stamped envelopes and offer to post these letters to children at some point in the future. Leave at least 2–3 weeks before sending them.

EXPANSION ACTIVITY 25.2. MY TREASURE CHEST

(See '20. Pirate's treasure parachute game'.)

Encourage the children to share their ideas about personal 'treasure' (see activity sheet 25.2). Sunil (aged 11), for example, came up with 'respecting others' as being an important treasure to have. Talk about the different treasure that each child chooses. Make regular times when they can 'find' something in their treasure chest. I have a collection of small boxes that children use for collecting gemstones (available from craft stores) to denote particular skills and qualities that they identify in themselves. Alternatively, each child could make a mini pirate's treasure chest with a posting slit on top so they can post cards with pictures or words on. These can then be retrieved when needed as reminders for future events, for example 'Remember that you are ace at planning' or 'Your sense of humour is really great'.

EXPANSION ACTIVITY 25.3. EMBLEMS OF SUCCESS

Draw the shape of a shield on a large piece of card. Divide the shield into four sections and draw different symbols or pictures in each section to show successful strategies for dealing with change. Possible strategies might be:

- talking with a friend
- asking for help to solve the difficulty
- listening to some relaxing music
- respecting and valuing myself
- finding a quiet space to 'chill out'.

Talk about

How can we keep ourselves motivated and feeling okay about big changes? (When new changes come along, we may have to go through some of the same processes to a lesser or greater degree, but think of this as recycling rather than starting from scratch.)

26. Completions

At the end of a series of group activity sessions, ask each child to write a short 'appreciation' for everyone else. This is simply done by having one piece of paper for each person passed around the group. I have found that appreciations can be more meaningful and personal than asking members to praise each other. For example, 'I really appreciate the support that you gave me when we worked together' or 'I appreciate your courage and determination in working on your goals' might be absorbed into the self-concept more easily than 'You are good at supporting others' or 'Well done for tackling your goals'. Participants read the sheet before they leave, but you could also offer to add them to each person's letter from the future (see activity sheet 25.1). It can be a great boost to receive this sort of feedback a few weeks later.

As an alternative, where I have used a lot of imagery throughout a course, I like to finish with an image. The children are invited to imagine that there is a large gift box in the middle of the floor and they can take away a gift from the whole group experience. They dip their hands into the box and allow the first image that comes to mind to be their gift. Sometimes it's a word or phrase (for example, 'Increased confidence') and sometimes it's an object, animal or colour ('A deckchair to help me to relax', 'A lion for courage', 'A blue blanket to remind me of all the support I have had'). One group that had gelled particularly well chose to give the gifts to each other.

A more 'high energy' activity might be appropriate for some groups, in which case you could use something fast and simple, like a Mexican Wave or passing a 'high five' around the circle.

VIII

Activity Sheets

The activity sheets in this section can be adapted for discussion or used as a basis for devising more complex activity sheets for older children.

Where possible, I suggest that you encourage children to draw rather than to write, and to work together rather than to sit quietly completing activity sheets on their own. This sharing and talking will not only help to foster collaborative, mutually respectful relationships, it also offers an opportunity for each child to enrich their understanding of the benefits of using imagery, being mindful and thinking creatively.

ACTIVITY SHEET 2.1. I AM ME

Imagine that you are your best friend talking about you. What would your friend say? For example, what might they say about what you like doing and what you are good at?

What might they say about what you *don't* like doing and about what worries you?

Begin with your name .... is:

ACTIVITY SHEET 3.1. THINGS I WOULD LIKE TO ACHIEVE

Draw or write about the things that you would like to achieve.

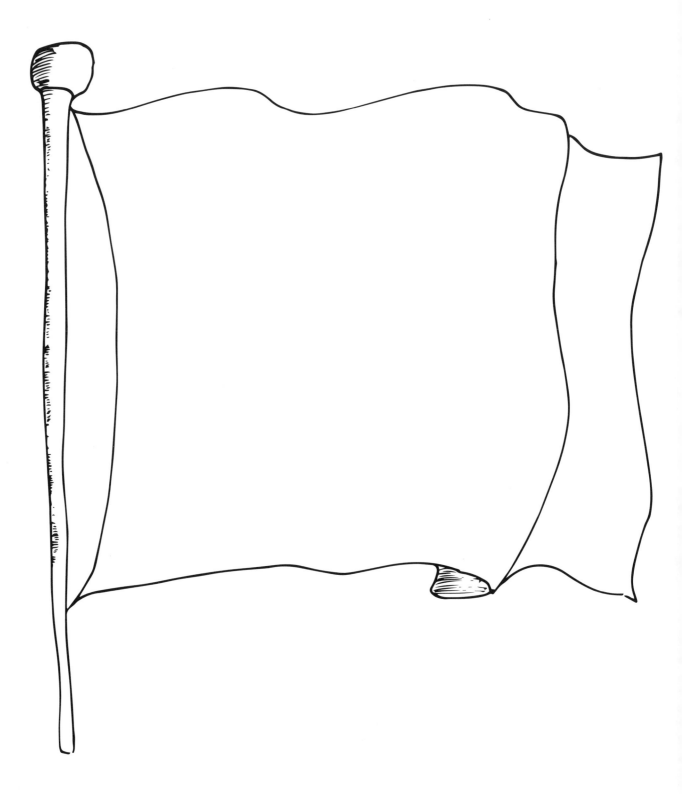

ACTIVITY SHEET 5.2. TALKING CATS

Let's imagine!

Imagine that you have a pet cat that can talk. This cat would like to know all the things that you do on school days. Make a list of (or draw) everything that you have to remember to do. Start your list with 'I wake up'.

....

....

....

....

....

....

You didn't have to wait until you had done each thing again before you wrote about it. You just imagined what you do each day.

Now you're giving your imagination a good work out!

ACTIVITY SHEET 5.3. BECOMING A CAT

Time to stretch your imagination a bit further.

Imagine that your pet cat wants to tell humans what it's like to be a cat.

What would it tell you? What does it like to do? What does it hate doing? What is it good at? What would it most like to happen? What does it think is the best thing about being a cat?

Close your eyes so that you can really begin to str-e-tch your imagination while you imagine having a conversation with your cat.

When you are ready, draw or write about what you imagined.

....

....

....

....

....

Imagine that!

ACTIVITY SHEET 6.1. HOW I FEEL

Having a feeling doesn't mean that you are always going to be like that.

Sam might feel shy when he goes to a new place where he doesn't know anyone, but that doesn't mean that he is always 'a shy person'. There are lots of times when Sam feels very confident.

Think of some times when you have felt some of these feelings. Draw or write about each of the feelings listed below.

A time when I felt very brave was

....

....

....

....

I felt excited when

....

....

....

....

I felt relaxed when

....

....

....

....

I felt nervous when

....

....

....

....

I felt angry when

....

....

....

....

I felt happy when

....

....

....

....

I felt disappointed when

....

....

....

....

ACTIVITY SHEET 6.2. MORE FEELINGS

Imagine what it might feel like to be a creature from outer space visiting a new planet for the first time.

Think of three words to describe how you would feel.

....

....

....

What are some of the important things you would need to know?

....

....

....

How would you find out about this new place?

....

....

....

What else would help you to feel okay about being in a new place?

....

....

....

Just imagine!

ACTIVITY SHEET 8.1. ANY MORE WORRIES?

Imagine that you could put your worries into a worry box and close the lid.

What do you think should happen to them then? Where would they go? Would anyone look at them? If so, who would it be? What would they do with them?

Draw or write about what happens.

ACTIVITY SHEET 8.2. THE WORRY TEAM

Imagine that you are part of a worry team.

This is a group of experts who spend their time inventing ways of getting rid of worries.

Make a list of things that you could do with worries. How inventive can you be?

QUIET PLEASE
worry team at work!

....

....

....

....

....

....

....

....

....

....

ACTIVITY SHEET 8.3. CATCHING WORRY THOUGHTS

Sometimes worry thoughts come into our minds and we hardly know they are there until they start to make us feel different.

You can learn to catch those thoughts before they make mischief.

When you notice a worry thought, imagine yourself catching it so you can have a good look at it.

Now that it is in your worry net you can see that it is just a worry thought. It doesn't need to be there!

Imagine yourself letting the worry thought fly away.

Write about or draw what happened to one of your worry thoughts when you let it go.

Just imagine!

ACTIVITY SHEET 9.2. IMPORTANT PEOPLE

Imagine that you are going to tell your class or group about all the people who are important to you.

What do you think the other children would like to know?

Draw a picture of one of your important people and write or draw about what they like to do. Why do you think they like to do this?

ACTIVITY SHEET 10.1. MY DISPLAY CABINET

Imagine that you have a special place where you can put important things on show for everyone to see.

Think of some important things about you that you would want to put on display.

ACTIVITY SHEET 10.2. THE MAGIC MIRROR

Look in the magic mirror. What can you see? What does the 'future you' look like?

ACTIVITY SHEET 10.3. APPRECIATION

What would you most like other people to know about you? What do you appreciate about yourself? What are your skills and assets?

Complete the 'asset jigsaw'.

ACTIVITY SHEET 12.1. JUNK THOUGHTS

Sometimes our thoughts are not very helpful to us.

Having these thoughts is a bit like eating too much junk food.

Think of some things that people might say to themselves that would stop them from learning a new skill, like playing football or riding a bike. These are junk thoughts.

....

....

Now think up some helpful thoughts. These are thoughts that help us to feel good. Having these thoughts is like eating healthy food.

....

....

If you were going to do something that might be difficult, what could you say to yourself before you start?

....

....

What could you say to yourself while you are in the situation?

....

....

What could you say to yourself afterwards?

....

....

ACTIVITY SHEET 15.2. THE BOOK OF WISDOM

Imagine that you have a special book, a book that knows the answers to lots of different questions. It is especially good at solving problems.

When you talk to this book it always listens, and sooner or later it always comes up with an answer. If you have a question or a problem to solve, write or draw about it here.

Imagine that you can ask *The Book of Wisdom* to help you. What does it tell you? Write or draw what it says.

....

....

....

....

....

....

....

....

Sometimes, the answer doesn't come straight away. Sometimes, you have to wait a few days and then, just when you least expect it, you'll know what to do! Imagine that!

ACTIVITY SHEET 19. IMAGINE MAKING A CHANGE

Are you about to make a change, like starting at a new school or moving to a new house?

Close your eyes and imagine that the change has already happened. What is different? What is happening? How do you feel? What will happen next? Draw or write about the change.

ACTIVITY SHEET 21.1. PREPARE TO DIVE!

When you look after yourself, you feel more ready to enjoy the easy, exciting or fun things in life and more ready to cope with those things that are especially difficult.

It's a bit like being ready to go diving in the sea.

Think about what you would need to have with you and what you would need to know if you were going diving.

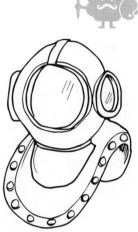

Before I go diving I would need to be

....

....

....

....

....

I would need to have

....

....

....

....

I would need to know

....

....

....

....

....

ACTIVITY SHEET 22.1. SKILLS FOR PROBLEM-SOLVING

See if you can 'solve' these problems:

Can you tie a knot in a piece of string without letting go of either end?

Can you draw a dot inside a circle without taking your pen off the paper?

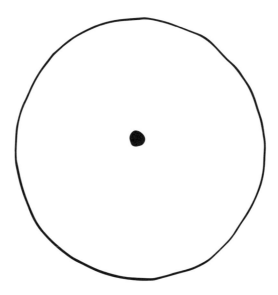

When you have worked out how to do these two tasks, take some time to think about the skills that you needed to solve the problems and make a list.

....

....

....

....

....

....

....

....

....

....

ACTIVITY SHEET 23.2. STEPS ALONG THE WAY

One thing I'd like to be able to do is:

....

....

These are the steps I need to take:

....

....

....

....

....

....

....

....

....

....

ACTIVITY SHEET 24.3. TAKING CARE OF MYSELF EVERY DAY

Imagine that you've had a very busy day at school and you feel quite tired.

Think of all the things that you could do now to help yourself to feel relaxed and refreshed. Draw or write about them here.

ACTIVITY SHEET 25.1. FUTURE ME

Take some time to write a special letter to yourself from the future, telling yourself what you did to reach your goal.

ACTIVITY SHEET 25.2. MY TREASURE CHEST

Let's imagine that you have a treasure chest that is full of all the great things about being you.

Can you imagine the chest? What is it made of? How big is it?

Imagine that every bit of treasure somehow shows us something special about you. Each piece of treasure has a label on it to show us what it is.

It would be a shame to keep all that treasure shut away in the chest all the time, don't you think?

Imagine that every day you go to your treasure chest and take a few things out to put on show so that we can all admire it.

What treasure will you choose today?

From my treasure chest today, I chose ....